III

NOTES

including
- *Historical Background*
- *Critical Introduction*
- *Brief Synopsis*
- *Scene-by-Scene Summaries and Commentaries*
- *Notes on Characters*
- *Review Questions*
- *Selected Bibliography*

by
James K. Lowers, Ph.D.
Department of English
University of Hawaii

INCORPORATED
LINCOLN, NEBRASKA 68501

Editor	Consulting Editor
Gary Carey, M.A.	*James L. Roberts, Ph.D.*
University of Colorado	*Department of English*
	University of Nebraska

ISBN 0-8220-0071-7
© Copyright 1966
by
Cliffs Notes, Inc.
All Rights Reserved
Printed in U.S.A.

1996 Printing

Cliffs Notes, Inc.   Lincoln, Nebraska

CONTENTS

RICHARD III

ON USING THE *NOTES*

Cliff's Notes are intended as an aid to the student in arriving at a mature understanding and appreciation of Shakespeare's *Richard III*. At no time should they be used as a substitute for the close reading—and re-reading—of the play itself.

It is true that any literary piece must be considered as an independent work of art. But it is no less true that quite often some background material must be acquired if the student is really to understand the work and to do justice to the author's intentions. Indeed, anyone who ignores what has been called the "Elizabethanness" of Shakespeare cannot hope to understand him.

As regards *Richard III,* all this means that the student should have sufficient knowledge of the historical events upon which the play is based and of how the dramatist made use of the records of those events. Further, he should have some knowledge of the Tudor attitude toward history and of the political, ethical, and religious doctrines which inform the work, since in *Richard III* history and tragedy meet. Finally, it is useful to know that Shakespeare followed certain literary traditions as relate to characterization of the protagonist, ingredients of tragedy, and style. To ignore such matters indicates that one is content to remain solely at the story level, which in this instance particularly, requires little effort and presents no challenge.

The student should read the play first at his normal rate in order to get the "story" and characters in mind. Then he should go back and read act by act critically, noting development of character, emergence of theme or themes, style, movement of the action to the climax and its fall to the catastrophe. It is here that the *Notes* should prove most helpful, providing as they do a summary of the action, critical commentary, and discussion of characters.

THE HISTORICAL BACKGROUND

Shakespeare's *Richard III* covers events in the latter years of the Wars of the Roses, that is, from the attainder and execution of George, Duke of Clarence, in 1478 to the defeat of Richard III at Bosworth Field in 1485. That war, a prolonged, intermittent conflict between the two noble houses of Lancaster and York which began in 1455, was closer to Shakespeare and

6

THE HOUSES OF YORK AND LANCASTER[1]

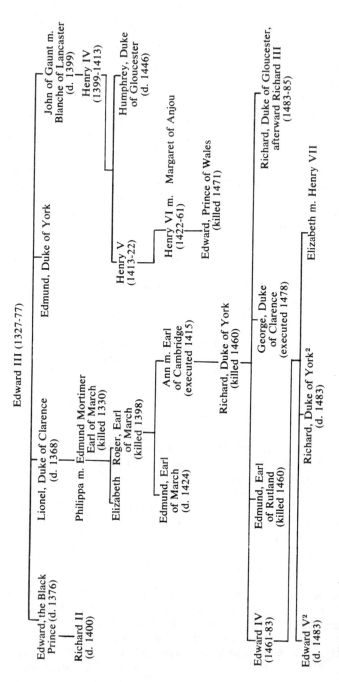

Edward III (1327-77)

Edward, the Black Prince (d. 1376)
Richard II (d. 1400)

Lionel, Duke of Clarence (d. 1368)
Philippa m. Edmund Mortimer Earl of March (killed 1330)
Roger, Earl of March (killed 1398)
Elizabeth
Edmund, Earl of March (d. 1424)

John of Gaunt m. Blanche of Lancaster (d. 1399)
Henry IV (1399-1413)
Henry V (1413-22)
Henry VI m. Margaret of Anjou (1422-61)
Edward, Prince of Wales (killed 1471)
Humphrey, Duke of Gloucester (d. 1446)

Edmund, Duke of York

Ann m. Earl of Cambridge (executed 1415)
Richard, Duke of York (killed 1460)
Edmund, Earl of Rutland (killed 1460)
Edward IV (1461-83)
George, Duke of Clarence (executed 1478)
Richard, Duke of Gloucester, afterward Richard III (1483-85)
Edward V[2] (d. 1483)
Richard, Duke of York[2] (d. 1483)
Elizabeth m. Henry VII

[1] Includes only the major persons.
[2] Shakespeare accepted the popular belief that Edward and Richard were murdered in the Tower of London.

his generation than are the Napoleonic wars to the present generation. On the throne of England when the dramatist wrote sat the granddaughter of Richmond, the first of the Tudors, who, it was firmly believed, was the godly savior of an England long torn by dissension and civil war. Particularly because throughout the sixteenth century England had reason to fear civil strife as well as foreign invasion, Elizabethans continued to manifest a keen interest in the historical events of the preceding century. As has been now well established, Shakespeare's generation viewed history as a mirror in which could be read lessons important to ruler and subject alike. Moreover, the chronicle histories which provided materials for Shakespeare's play were written with a Tudor bias, presenting and interpreting character and event from the point of view accepted as orthodox in sixteenth-century England.

Since constant reference to earlier events in the conflict are found in *Richard III*, it is desirable briefly to review the story of the Wars of the Roses, which lasted for thirty years and in which some eighty princes of the blood, many members of the nobility, and at least 100,000 commoners were slain. This was the dynastic struggle between the house of York and the house of Lancaster. Actually, the Lancastrians never adopted the Red Rose as their symbol, it having been used first by Henry Tudor (Richmond) in 1485.

Head of the White Rose party was Richard Plantagenet, third Duke of York, whose claim to the throne was an impressive one. On his mother's side of the family, he was descended from Lionel, Duke of Clarence, elder brother of John of Gaunt, from whom the Lancastrians were descended. Unfortunately for Richard, however, parliament had declared for the younger line, which had the advantage of straight descent through the males.

Richard of York was able to capitalize upon Henry VI's notorious weakness as a ruler and his misfortunes. Following Jack Cade's Rebellion (1450) he was hailed as a popular champion, particularly because of his opposition to the Duke of Somerset, who conducted affairs for the king. There was even a proposal that he be recognized as heir to the throne, the first suggestion of the devastating quarrel which became known as the Wars of the Roses. Taking some liberty with history, Shakespeare dramatized the origin of these two hostile parties in *Henry VI, Part Two*, and continued the story of events in the third part, wherein the Yorkists emerged triumphant.

By the year 1453, when Henry VI became quite ill, the Duke of York succeeded in getting control of the government and was appointed "Protector and Defender of the Realm" by parliament. But the king recovered late in the next year, and York was replaced by his rival Somerset. He did not remain quiet for long. When a council was summoned to make provisions "for the safety of the King against his enemies," the duke led a force of his supporters in a march on London. Somerset, joined by the king and a host of nobles, led an army from London to meet the threat, and the two forces met at St. Albans. The Wars of the Roses had begun. Somerset was killed, and Margaret of Anjou, Henry's energetic queen, emerged as head of the Lancastrian party. During the next four years, England experienced a period of restiveness before warfare broke out again. Although York was supported by the powerful Earl of Warwick, head of the house of Neville, the Yorkists were defeated and the duke himself fled to Ireland.

But King Henry's government, now controlled by Margaret and her council, proved anything but efficient. Faced by poverty and disaster, the average Englishman yearned for the return of Richard of York. In June, 1460, Warwick and Edward, Earl of March, the duke's eldest son, moved on London and were joined by York, who again claimed the crown. This time parliament ruled that the head of the house of York should be heir to the hapless Henry VI. But Margaret was not to be repressed. She succeeded in mustering a strong force in the north and met the Yorkists at Wakefield. In this battle, the duke lost his life. And, since Edward was just a youth of eighteen, Warwick became the head of the White Rose party. In the next year the new leader was overwhelmingly defeated in the second Battle of St. Albans. Nevertheless, Warwick managed to join forces with Edward and to occupy London. Thus Margaret lost the fruits of her victory. Young Edward was declared king by the citizens and lords of Yorkshire and did not hesitate to take the throne, although this did not constitute a legal election.

Subsequent events worked in Edward's favor. Margaret's Lancastrian forces were defeated near Towton in York on March 29, 1461. Henry and his son fled to Scotland. By 1464, Edward was full master of England. Nevertheless, his position was jeopardized by his marriage to Elizabeth, a widowed daughter of Richard Woodville. Warwick, his chief supporter, was enraged, not only because the Woodvilles were of Lancastrian connection but because Warwick himself had all but completed a plan for the English monarch to marry the sister of Louis XI of France. Edward IV aggravated matters by favoring his wife's relatives at the expense of the Nevilles. Henry had returned to England in 1465 and had been placed in the Tower of London. Not long thereafter, however, the former king was released, and Edward was forced to flee to Holland. Thanks to the support of Charles of Burgundy, Edward was able to muster a force and to return to England. Once more the unfortunate Henry was imprisoned, and Warwick's army was defeated, the earl himself being slain. To cap all this, the Lancastrians suffered a devastating defeat at Tewkesbury on May 4, 1471. Margaret was taken prisoner and the young prince was put to death. Henry VI was reported to have died "of pure displeasure and melancholy," but in all probability Edward IV ordered that he be put to death.

For *The Tragedy of Richard III,* Shakespeare picked up the story with the attainder of the Duke of Clarence, who had married a daughter of Warwick and had served his father-in-law from 1469 to 1471, and who had been involved constantly in quarrels with the king and with his other brother, Richard of Gloucester. Inevitably, there are frequent references to earlier events in the play.

A CRITICAL INTRODUCTION

The history of this period dating from the reign of Richard II to the defeat of Richard III at Bosworth Field in 1485 was dramatized in two tetralogies. The first includes *Richard II* (1595), the two *Henry IV* plays (1597-98), and *Henry V* (1599).[1] In these plays Shakespeare presented the tragic fortunes of Richard II which culminated in his deposition and murder: the rebellions which harassed the reign of the usurper and regicide, Henry IV; and the triumph of Henry V, who escaped punishment in this world for the sins of his father because he engaged English forces in a war against a foreign enemy, France, winning his famous victories. The second tetralogy includes the three *Henry VI* plays (1590-92)[2] and *Richard III* (1593). Obviously, the latter plays predate those comprising the first tetralogy, but there is sufficient evidence, external and internal, that Shakespeare, like his contemporaries, saw in the deposition of Richard II, a lawful anointed ruler, the source of England's troubles during the entire period. This is a point worth keeping in mind because it makes understandable why the descendants of Lancastrian Henry IV as well as the members of the Yorkist party should be made to suffer grievously.

The first Quarto of *Richard III* (1597) provides the only external evidence for dating the play, but internal evidence is sufficiently great to point to the earlier date of composition cited above. Certainly the close relation to *Henry VI, Part Three,* wherein the character of Richard of Gloucester is

[1]Here and elsewhere the generally accepted dates of composition are given.

[2]Whether Shakespeare was actually the sole author of the *Henry VI* plays is still disputed, but there is little doubt that they are substantially his works.

fully established, indicates that the play was written soon after that chronicle history reached an appreciative public. The style is unmistakably that of early Shakespeare – the poet-dramatist who was still under the influence of his predecessors. As Sir Edmund K. Chambers pointed out (*William Shakespeare,* Vol. I. 1930, p. 302), it is a highly mannered, rhetorical style marked by frequent exclamations, violent and vituperative speeches, cumulative passages of parallel lines with parisonic endings and beginnings, as in these lines spoken by Queen Margaret:

> I had an Edward, till a Richard kill'd him;
> I had a husband, till a Richard kill'd him:
> Thou hadst an Edward, till a Richard kill'd him;
> Thou hadst a Richard, till a Richard kill'd him.
>
> (IV.iv.40-43)

The elaborate imagery, repetitions, quibbles, and conceits in the wooing scene (I.ii) provide good examples of the early playwright who is rather pleased with his cleverness rather than wholly concerned with character portrayal. All of these stylistic devices may be found in later Shakespeare, to be sure, but never in such abundance. Significant also is the fact that the blank verse in this play is largely end-stopped – that is, there is a grammatical or rhetorical pause at the end of most lines rather than an overrunning of sense from one line to another, which gives a more naturalness to the discourse. The student will find it useful to read aloud and to compare Richard's opening soliloquy with any of those in the late tragedies to appreciate the stylistic difference.

Certain elements of style in *Richard III* are to be traced to the Roman dramatist Seneca, and these merit notice here. The ten tragedies attributed to Seneca were available in translation by 1581; indeed the first dates from 1559. These had great influence upon many of Shakespeare's predecessors and contemporaries. The tone and temper of the Roman's works, his sensationalism and moralizing, his stress on the tragedy of the individual had wide appeal. Comparatively ignorant of the Greek tragic writers, Shakespeare's generation found in Seneca inspiration and, to an appreciable extent, the model for their own tragedies. As for style, the self-revealing soliloquy, the long speeches characterized by full-blown rhetoric, the often epigrammatic alternating lines of speech and reply called *stichomythia* (as in the dialogue between Richard and Anne beginning "I would I knew thy heart," I.ii.193 ff.) all found a place in Elizabethan tragedy, including *Richard III.* Likewise with reference to the sensationalism in developing the theme of murder and revenge. Indeed Elizabethans went beyond Seneca, in whose plays violence is reported or described, not presented onstage.

More often than not, such violence was depicted before the eyes of Elizabethan audiences. Among the Senecan trappings of tragedy are ghosts, foreboding dreams, signs and omens of impending catastrophe — all of which appear in *Richard III.*

With the stress on the individual, Seneca pointed the way to the one-man play, the drama in which the protagonist almost completely dominates the action. Because Shakespeare followed this lead he achieved a unity theretofore unknown in chronicle history plays. The *Henry VI* plays, for example, are notably epic in structure. The shifted emphasis to the titular hero makes justifiable the title *The Tragedy of Richard III.* This brings us to the hero-villain and the second line of influence, a knowledge of which adds appreciably to an understanding of the play. The reference is to the stage Machiavel. It has been argued that Machiavelli, author of *The Prince* (1513), was actually an early political idealist seeking to unify Italy by appealing to the ambitions of the Renaissance princes. But for most Elizabethans the Machiavellian was practically equated with the Devil. Political cunning, overreaching by diplomacy and intrigue came to be known as Machiavellianism, the philosophy of which seems to have been that the end justified the means, however cruel they may be. Christopher Marlowe brought the Machiavellian villain to the stage in his *The Jew of Malta* and *The Massacre of Paris.* In Shakespeare's *Henry VI, Part Three* (III.iii. 124-95), Richard of Gloucester soliloquizes, identifying himself as one whose criminal ambitions will lead him to "set the murderous Machiavel to school." He thus early emerged as the complete Machiavellian villain-hero. The specific characteristics of this type must await our comments on Richard himself.

The dramatized story of Richard had wide appeal, and Shakespeare's play was not the only one based upon his career. Other versions were performed in the public theaters and at Cambridge University. As late as 1602 Ben Jonson started to write a play entitled *Richard Crookback.* It is not only the fact that the evil character of Richard was bound to be fascinating for so many and that the accompanying sensationalism had quite as great an appeal; English history had its special attraction for the Elizabethans. And was not the queen's grandfather the man who defeated Richard and established the Tudor dynasty? Most Englishmen were deeply interested in plays which dealt with the dynastic question, for Elizabeth I never had named her successor. Dissension and civil war, it was feared, might well follow the death of the aging queen.

Richard Burbage, distinguished tragedian in Shakespeare's company, won wide acclaim for his creation of the title role, and the king's exclamation "A horse! A horse! My kingdom for a horse!" was much admired and was imitated by Shakespeare's fellow dramatists. Further evidence of popularity is the fact that no less than six Quarto editions of the play were published between 1597 and 1622. Throughout the years it has remained a favorite among the history plays. If it must relinquish first place to *Henry IV* (thanks especially to the presence of the incomparable Falstaff), *Richard III* has held its own very well. During the nineteenth and well into the twentieth centuries it was often the choice of leading actors because the titular hero dominates the action and because the rhetorical school of acting still flourished. There are other reasons, of course. Bernard Shaw, reviewing Sir Henry Irving's production for the *Saturday Review* in 1896, wrote as follows:

> The world being yet little better than a mischievous school-boy, I am afraid it cannot be denied that Punch and Judy holds the field still as the most popular of dramatic entertainments. And of all its versions...Shakespear's Richard III is the prince of Punches: he delights Man by provoking God, and dies unrepentant and game to the last...

This is sound criticism. Especially, Shaw's remarks stress the fact that the spectacle of the unconscionable, dedicated sinner, one possessed with inordinate ability and endowed with a fine wit, is irresistibly fascinating.

Quite accurately the blank verse of *Richard III* has been described as "simple." As has been stated above it is early Shakespearean blank verse. But already the distinctive Shakespearean accents are noticeable. It would do the playwright an injustice to underestimate the effects he attains or to dismiss the style as predominantly one of rant, bombast, fustian. In the first place, the standards of realism, as we understand the term today, are no more applicable to the style of the play than they are to much of the action and the portrayal of character. Surely no one would step forth and, voicing his thoughts aloud, declare that he is determined to be a villain. Nor would it be possible for the most gifted individual to effect the complete *volte-face* which we witness when Richard, first excoriated by the grief-stricken widow of Edward, Prince of Wales, succeeds in winning the hand of that lady even as she follows the hearse of the murdered Henry VI. Shakespeare did not offer all this as a slice of life. His audiences were familiar with the story of Richard conceived as the arch-villain whose nemesis was the first of the Tudors. It had been told by Sir Thomas More, whose vividly written tragical history in prose was printed complete in 1557; and More's work had been used by the chronicle historians, Richard Grafton, Edward Hall, and Raphael Holinshed, the latter being Shakespeare's chief source.

In *Richard III* one does not have any great difficulty in finding lines which manifest the sure touch of a superior poet. Consider, for example, the fourth one of the opening scene: "In the deep bosom of the ocean buried." Or take the following memorable lines spoken by Queen Elizabeth, whose daughter Richard wishes to marry:

> Send to her by the man that slew her brothers
> A pair of bleeding hearts; thereon engrave
> Edward and York: then haply will she weep.
> Therefore present to her, — as sometimes Margaret
> Did thy father, steep'd in Rutland's blood, —
> A handkerchief; which, say to her did drain
> The purple sap from her sweet brother's body;
> And bid her wipe her weeping eyes withal.
>
> (IV.iv.271-78)

Finally, listen to Gloucester's reply when he is warned to beware of falling:

> Our aery buildeth in the cedar's top
> And dallies with the wind and scorns the sun. (I.iii.264-65)

These are as attractive as poetry as they are dramatically effective.

All this is not to deny that the formal verbal patterning seems to be excessive and to pose a special problem for modern readers and members of the audience. Yet such a style is consistent with the basic pattern of retributive justice which provides the major theme of this historical tragedy — God's inexorable punishment visited upon those guilty of the heinous crimes of murder and perjury. The first example is found in Act I, scene ii, when the distraught Lady Anne laments the death of Henry VI, the "holy king":

> O cursed be the hand that made these holes!
> Cursed be the heart that had the heart to do it!
> Cursed the blood that let his blood from hence. (14-16)

The device is especially prominent in the speeches of Queen Margaret, one example of which has been quoted above.

In keeping with the major theme, Richard of Gloucester functions as the Scourge of God before he himself is scourged for his heinous crimes. If Shakespeare remained faithful to the received interpretation of Gloucester's character, he nevertheless manifested his originality and ability as a dramatist throughout the play. Most of the best known speeches are his creations. These include the opening soliloquy, Clarence's impassioned outbursts, and the long tirades of Queen Margaret. Similarly with reference to much of the action and shorter dialogue. The wooing scene between Richard and Anne, for example, is original with Shakespeare, as is the ironic exchange between the titular hero and the young Duke of York. If Holinshed gave him the lead for depicting the villain's hypocritical display of religiosity when the mayor appeared and when the well-schooled Buckingham offered Richard the crown (III.vii), it remained for Shakespeare to make the most of the hint; for the chronicle historian reported no more than that Richard appeared "with a bishop on every hand of him."

In order to concentrate our interest, the poet-dramatist crowds into the space of a few days the funeral of Henry VI (1471), the murder of Clarence (1478), and the death of Edward IV (1483). The historic time from the burial of Henry VI to the Battle of Bosworth Field (1485) was more than fourteen years. The *dramatic* time was some eleven or twelve days with four intervals—between I.ii and I.iii; II.iii and II.iv; IV.v and V.i; and V.ii. Shakespeare thus achieved a degree of unity unknown to the episodic *Henry VI* plays and helped to justify the title *The Tragedy of Richard III*.

LEADING CHARACTERS IN *RICHARD III*

Richard, Duke of Gloucester, Afterward Richard III

Richard was the youngest son of the third Duke of York who was killed at Wakefield in 1460. In *Henry VI, Part Two,* and more particularly in *Henry VI, Part Three,* he first appeared as a vigorous Yorkist and warrior. But then he emerged in the latter play as "hard-favored Richard," "a ragged fatal rock," and "an undigested lump"—each phrase suggesting that his deformity was the reflection of his profoundly evil character. As has been stated above, he identified himself as one who would outdo Machiavel, that is, as a super-Machiavel, in his efforts to win the crown of England. The basic characteristics of the stage Machiavel of Elizabethan drama are indeed his: boundless ambition, egotistical action, masterly dissembling, defiance of God, great if misguided intellectuality. Yet it has been well observed by C. H. Tawney that "Richard would be intolerable from an aesthetic point of view if he did not excel all the characters that surround him in prudence, energy..., consistent courage, quite as much as he surpasses them in ruthless cruelty and selfishness." Moreover, Richard, denounced as "hell's black intelligencer," "that foul defacer of God's handiwork," and "that black bottl'd spider, that foul bunch-back'd toad," possesses a sardonic wit and a fine sense of irony.

King Edward IV

Edward IV, the eldest son of the Duke of York, ruled England from 1461 to 1483. Anything but a weak ruler, he nevertheless had his difficulties

First, his marriage to Elizabeth Woodville, which had led to the disaffection of the Earl of Warwick, the chief support of the Yorkists, was a continuing source of trouble, for he tended to favor her relatives at the expense of the Nevilles and other families the members of which had favored the Yorkist cause. Second, his reputation as a loose gallant, and particularly his relationship with the beautiful Jane Shore, daughter of a London goldsmith, made possible charges that his mistress adversely influenced his conduct of public affairs. Finally, a well-known clergyman, one Dr. Ralph Shaw, referred to in Act III, scene v, 104, publicly charged that, in the words of the chronicler Robert Fabyan (*The Concordance of Histories*, 1516), "the children of King Edward IV were not legitimate, nor rightful heirs of the crown." This charge was based upon the widely circulated story that Edward had been secretly married before his union to Lady Elizabeth Grey and that his first wife was still alive. Richard of Gloucester of the play capitalized upon all three of these sources of difficulty. Edward appears in *Richard III* as the ailing ruler, one actually on his deathbed. His great concern is to quiet dissension and to insure the orderly succession of the crown.

George, Duke of Clarence

The third son of the Duke of York and brother to Edward IV and Richard of Gloucester first appeared in *Henry VI, Part Three*. In that play he is described as a "quicksand of deceit" and for good reason. Clarence had been elevated to a dukedom by his newly crowned brother after the defeat of Queen Margaret's forces near Towton. But he joined the disgruntled Warwick and was betrothed to the earl's second daughter. It was to Clarence as well as to Warwick that the liberated Henry VI resigned his government, while Edward IV was forced to find haven on the Continent. But once more Clarence changed loyalties, removing the red rose from his helmet and proclaiming himself to be the "mortal foe" of Warwick, who denounced him as "perjur'd and unjust." In *Henry VI, Part Three*, Clarence also is made to join Edward and Richard in stabbing Prince Edward, son of Henry VI and Margaret of Anjou. History records that he was constantly involved in quarrels with his older brother.

Henry, Duke of Buckingham

Buckingham inherited his title from Humphrey Stafford, one of the commanders of the royal forces at the first Battle of St. Albans. Understandably Queen Margaret first praises him as blameless. Holinshed described him as "easie to handle," and for a time so the Richard of this play found him to be. To Richard he was the "deep-revolving, witty [i.e., cunning]

Buckingham" who functioned as the villain-hero's Warwick, or king-maker. But unlike Warwick, Buckingham is depicted as, to use another of Richard's phrases, one "of many simple gulls," susceptible to gross flattery and convinced that his fortunes will be advanced if he serves the ambitious Richard. Too late he learns that he has judged falsely.

Henry Tudor, Earl of Richmond, Afterward King Henry VII

Richmond was the nearest male representative of the Lancastrians. He was the son of Owen Tudor and Katherine, the widow of Henry V. He was also the lineal descendant, by Katherine Swynford, of John of Gaunt. Henry thus inherited the Lancastrian line, although he was debarred by parliament from the throne. Nevertheless, he had many English supporters, and when he escaped to France after the Battle of Tewkesbury, he bided his time for a while and then issued a manifesto calling upon Englishmen to join him in crushing Richard, "the unnatural tyrant who bore rule over them." Thanks to his marriage to Elizabeth, daughter of Edward IV, he was able to unite the dynastic claims of both parties. Shakespeare followed his sources in depicting Henry as the God-sent savior of England.

Queen Margaret, widow of Henry VI

She appeared with increasing prominence in each of the *Henry VI* plays. Daughter of the Duke of Anjou, titular King of Naples, and niece of Charles VII, she was a determined, strong-minded woman who offered a complete contrast to her pious, well-meaning, weak husband. When the Duke of Somerset was slain in the first Battle of St. Albans (1455) Margaret came forward as head of the royal party prosecuting the civil war against the Yorkists. After her defeat at Tewkesbury, she was imprisoned, but was then released on payment of a ransom by France. Actually she died in 1482 but survived in Shakespeare's play, where she functions as a terrifying chorus, a symbolic figure standing for the doom of the house of York.

Elizabeth, Queen to Edward IV

Elizabeth was the widowed daughter of Sir Richard Woodville and patron of the Woodville faction, who were of Lancastrian connection. In the play, this faction is represented by her brother, Earl Rivers, and her two sons by her first husband, the Marquis of Dorset and Lord Grey. In *Richard III* she appears to yield to Richard's blandishments; but since she survived to see her daughter become Queen of England, it may be questioned that she was the "relenting fool and shallow changing woman" described by Richard.

Lady Anne

The widow of Edward, Prince of Wales, son of Henry VI, was the daughter of the Earl of Warwick and thus a Neville. The fact that she possessed much property is not the sole reason why Richard of Gloucester should have turned ardent wooer. The Neville connection fitted in with his ambitions to gain the crown.

The Duchess of York

The mother of King Edward IV, Clarence, and Richard was the daughter of Ralph Neville, first Earl of Northumberland. Since her husband first made his bid for the crown, she had endured "accursed and wrangling days," surviving not only the Duke of York's death, but also the deaths of her sons. She also endured the agonizing realization that Richard was one who was "damned," one who had come "on earth to make [her] earth a hell" and who deserved his mother's "most grievous curse."

William, Lord Hastings

Hastings, an adherent to the Yorkist cause, was described as "a noble man" by Holinshed. He served as lord chamberlain to Edward IV, but was opposed by Queen Elizabeth because the king favored him. Like Buckingham, then, he was at odds with the Woodvilles. Holinshed links him with Buckingham as one whom Richard first considered as "easie to handle." It is difficult to avoid the conclusion that Hastings was obtuse. When Richard arrested members of the queen's faction, he decided that the action was necessary to the safety of the realm, and he was confident that his own position was secure. Obtuse or not, he emerged as one representing loyal nobility, faithful to the throne rather than to one faction or another. Inevitably, Richard denounced him as a traitor and saw to it that he was put to death without a trial, as Shakespeare's sources reported.

BRIEF SYNOPSIS

The wars being over, Richard of Gloucester determines to gain the throne occupied by his brother, Edward IV. He first manages to turn Edward against the Duke of Clarence, who is imprisoned in the Tower on the charge of treason. Next, he wins the hand of Lady Anne, even as she follows the hearse bearing the body of the murdered Henry VI. As part of his plan, Richard succeeds in convincing Hastings and Buckingham that the queen and her faction are to blame for Clarence's imprisonment. Hired murderers carry out his instructions to put Clarence to death.

Richard joins the other members of the hostile factions in solemnly vowing in the presence of the dying Edward to hold the peace. The remorseful king learns that Clarence has been put to death before he himself dies. When the young Prince Edward is sent for from Ludlow to be crowned,

Richard moves quickly to meet this turn of events. Buckingham, now Richard's "second self," promises to separate the prince from the queen's kindred. Lord Rivers, Lord Grey, and Sir Thomas Vaughan are imprisoned by Richard and are executed. The frightened queen seeks sanctuary for her son.

With a great display of courtesy and devotion, Richard has Prince Edward and his brother lodged in the Tower. Finding that Hastings remains loyal to the prince, the villain-hero denounces him as a traitor and orders his execution. Soon thereafter Rivers, Grey, and Vaughan meet like fates. Next, Richard convinces the Lord Mayor of London that he has acted only for the security of the realm. He has Buckingham slander the dead Edward, implying that the late king's children are illegitimate and that Edward himself was basely born. When citizens of London, headed by the lord mayor, offer him the crown, Richard accepts it with pretended reluctance. Arrangements are made for his coronation.

The despairing queen-mother fails in an attempt to visit her sons in the Tower just before Richard is crowned. To secure his position, the new king suggests to Buckingham that the young princes be put to death. But the duke falters at the thought of such a monstrous deed. Dorset, it is learned, has fled to Britanny to join Henry, Earl of Richmond. This turn of events does not deter King Richard. He has rumors spread that his wife is mortally ill; he arranges a lowly match for Margaret, Clarence's daughter; he imprisons Clarence's son; he engages Sir James Tyrrel to undertake the murder of the little princes. Buckingham, now treated disdainfully and denied the promised earldom of Hereford, resolves to join Richmond. Anne dies, and Richard offers himself as husband for his niece, Elizabeth of York. Richmond lands at Milford at the head of a mighty army. Joined by many nobles, he marches inland to claim the throne. Buckingham is captured and slain.

The two armies meet at Bosworth Field, and the two leaders are encamped on either side. That night the ghosts of Richard's victims appear, indicting him and prophesying his defeat. In contrast, Richmond has "fair-boding dreams" and is assured that "God and good angels" stand ready to assist him. Both Richard and Richmond address their troops before the battle begins. Richard fights courageously but is overcome and slain in personal combat with Richmond, who accepts the crown and proposes to marry Elizabeth of York, thus ending the dissension between the two great factions.

SUMMARIES AND COMMENTARIES
ACT I – SCENE 1

Summary

Appearing on a London street, Richard, Duke of Gloucester, soliloquizes, providing much exposition and revealing a great deal about himself, The long years of the Lancastrian supremacy are over, and the house of York, like the rising sun, is now in the ascendant. Those who have distinguished themselves in the grim arts of war are relaxing in the pleasure of love. Richard refers particularly to his brother Edward IV.

The thought of his handsome brother reminds Richard of his own deformity. He has one withered arm and a hunched back and so concludes that he is unfit for love. Therefore he will play the villain. The first of his wicked plots is already under way: he has told Edward about a prophecy which says that someone with a name beginning with "G" will murder Edward's heirs. The king has taken this to mean his other brother, George, Duke of Clarence.

Richard's thoughts are interrupted by the entrance of Clarence, who is guarded by Brackenbury, Lieutenant of the Tower, much to the apparent surprise and concern of Richard. Clarence explains that he is being sent to the Tower because Edward has listened to the prophecy about the letter "G." Richard is quick to attribute the king's action to the fact that he is ruled by his wife, Elizabeth Woodville, who with her brother had had Lord Hastings imprisoned. He declares that the king's blood relatives and supporters are no longer safe.

Richard and Clarence then talk disparagingly of the queen and of the king's mistress, Jane Shore, whom they accuse of ruling the kingdom by gossip. Brackenbury intervenes, not wishing to overhear such dangerous talk. Insisting that there is no question of treasonable discourse, Richard then demonstrates his wit and sense of irony as he slyly speaks of the "noble Queen" and catalogues the attractions of Jane Shore. With resignation, Clarence agrees to accompany Brackenbury, and his brother assures him that he will either deliver him from prison or take his place as a prisoner. Alone, however, Richard restates his determination to have his brother's soul sent to heaven.

Hastings, newly released from prison, enters. He vows that he will avenge himself upon those responsible for his imprisonment, and brings news that the king is ill. Richard blames this illness on Edward's self-indulgence and promises to follow Hastings to his bedside. The scene ends with another soliloquy in which Richard elaborates his evil plans. Clarence must be disposed of at once, before King Edward's death. Then Richard will marry Warwick's daughter Anne, though he had killed her husband, Edward, Prince of Wales, and her father-in-law, Henry VI. He explains that the marriage will further his ends. Aware that his plans are barely started, he goes off to take definite action.

Commentary

In having the titular hero appear first onstage and soliloquize at length, Shakespeare was following a convention that he later outgrew. In the more mature plays, the way is prepared by means of expository dialogue before the tragic hero's entrance. This opening soliloquy accomplishes all that a prologue would, and subtlety is the last thing to look for here. Gloucester paints himself as an unnatural monster. He is lame, ugly, "rudely stamped." A common belief of the time was that the warped moral being of the individual was often reflected in his physical appearance.

In the first two lines is found a typical Shakespearean play upon a word —the word *sun* in this instance. Edward IV was the son of the Duke of York and bore a sun on his armorial crest. Metaphorically, he was the bright sun of the Yorkist party, now in the ascendant. And, of course, the sun is a well-known symbol of royalty. Notice how skillfully Shakespeare sustains the sun metaphor:

> Why, I, in this weak piping time of peace
> Have no delight to pass away the time,
> Unless to see *my shadow in the sun,*
> And descant on mine own deformity.   (24-27)

As a dedicated Machiavellian, he takes pride in his deviousness and treachery, and emerges as one filled with envy (a Deadly Sin) and motivated by criminal ambition. The adjective "piping" and the verb "descant" relate to the shepherd's life, the shepherd being a familiar symbol of the tranquility which Richard scorns.

Already the action has begun to rise. We know about Gloucester's ambition; we know what is the first step he has taken to realize that ambition. When he protests to Clarence, "Alack, my lord, that fault is none of yours," we witness the first display of Machiavellian dissembling. His exchange with the apprehensive Brackenbury provides a good example of his wit and gift for irony. These two qualities are further illustrated by his use of "abjects" for "subjects" and by his expression of deep concern for his brother:

> Meantime, this deep disgrace in brotherhood
> Touches me deeper than you can imagine.   (111-12)

"Disgrace in brotherhood" has three levels of meaning: the unnatural action of a brother (Edward IV); my own underhanded behavior; disgrace to a brother (Clarence). Similarly, the word "lie" in the final words to Clarence means, on the surface, that Gloucester will take Clarence's place in prison; but it also means that the villain-hero will tell more lies about his brother.

With the arrival of Lord Hastings, two circumstances which may work to Richard's advantage are revealed. First, Hastings is determined to avenge himself upon those who were responsible for his imprisonment; therefore, Richard may find him a useful ally. Second, King Edward is "sickly, weak, and melancholy." The reader will not miss the irony of Gloucester's voiced reaction: "Now, by Saint Paul, this is bad indeed." He will make use of such sacred oaths frequently and thus provide further evidence of his hypocrisy. Despite his outward show of loyalty and fraternal love, he does not fail to indict Edward as one whose "evil diet" has "overmuch consumed his royal person." What with the Woodville faction alienating powerful nobles like Hastings, and with the ruler incapacitated as the supposed result of a dissolute life, a way may be found for Richard to seize power. His plan to marry Lady Anne, if carried out successfully, will work to his advantage. But immediately all depends upon what happens to Clarence and to Edward.

A recapitulation of what has been accomplished in this first scene should be useful. Richard is presented as by far the most important character in the play. The present situation in the kingdom is made clear: Edward IV, the ailing ruler, appears to be dominated by his wife, and the older nobles are resentful. The relation between the three sons of the Duke of York is set forth: Edward is a dying king; Clarence a traitor and perjurer; Richard the destroyer of his brother. The scene also provides the motives for Richard's villainy and shows that by his lying words he will be able to stir up more dissension. Finally, the scene prepares for the courtship of Lady Anne.

ACT I — SCENE 2

Summary

Lady Anne, second daughter of the Earl of Warwick, appears onstage, following the funeral cortege of the slain Henry VI, whom she identifies as her father-in-law. She is escorting the body of this "holy King," last great member of the house of Lancaster, to Chertsey in Surrey for burial. Making reference also to herself as the wife of Edward, the "slaughtered son" of the dead ruler, she calls upon the ghost of Henry to hear her lamentations. Heaping curses on the murderer she implores God to punish him: Let any child of his be born prematurely and prove to be monstrous; if he marry, let his wife endure the misery of his death, even as Anne herself now suffers.

At this point Richard enters and violently stops the procession in order to speak to Anne. She denounces him vehemently and utters the prophetic cry, "Thou hast made the happy earth thy hell." She points out that King Henry's wounds have started to bleed again as a result of Richard's presence. Gloucester appeals to her charity. In a dialogue of quick and studied repartee, she heaps more curses upon him, while he parries with flattering words and begs for the chance to explain himself. Though she scorns him and even spits upon him, he is not to be deterred. He presses his suit, declaring that if he was guilty of Henry's and Edward's death, he had been motivated solely by his desire to possess her beauty. When she denounces him as a "foul toad" which infects her eyes, Richard insists that the beauty of her eyes makes him weep—he, who remained dry-eyed when his brother Rutland and his father had been slain. This recital merely excites her scorn; so he bares his bosom, gives her his sword, and—admitting that he indeed killed Henry and Prince Edward—invites her to kill him. When Anne refuses to be his executioner, he urges her to tell him to kill himself, but to do so not in rage. At last Anne is in some doubt and she says: "I would I knew thy heart." Richard is quick to press his advantage and prevails on her to accept a ring. When she takes it, she states that she promises nothing in return. Nevertheless, when he asks her to repair to Crosby Place, his London residence, and there to wait for him while he buries King Henry with his "repentant tears," she promptly agrees to do so.

Alone, Richard gloats over this conquest of Lady Anne made when the odds were so great against him—the fact that she changed from a mood of venemous hate to one of ready acquiescence and found him "to be a marvelous proper man," particularly in contrast to her dead husband, whom he had killed at Tewkesbury some three months earlier. He reveals his plan to "have her...but not keep her long." In view of his success so far, he finds that his deformity pleases him.

Commentary

There has been some dispute as regards the question of whether or not Lady Anne Neville actually had been married to Prince Edward, although there is no question as to the betrothal of the two. Margaret of Anjou did object at first to the proposed marriage of her son to Warwick's second daughter; but, perhaps under pressure of Louis XI, she finally gave her consent. Edward and Anne were married on December 13, 1470, by the

Grand Vicar of Bayeux. The queen, however, left herself as free as possible to disavow or annul the marriage later. It is doubtful that the young couple ever lived together as man and wife. (Cf. Paul M. Kendall, *Richard the Third,* New York, 1956, p. 123).

When the dramatist has Anne point out that the wounds of the dead King Henry have started to bleed again, he makes effective use of the popular belief that the wounds of a murdered man bleed in the presence of the murderer.

It will be noticed that Anne repeatedly addresses Richard as "thou" and "thee," whereas the villain-hero addresses her as "you." Anne shifts to the latter form when she tacitly indicates her willingness to favor Richard's suit: "Well, well, put up your sword." The familiar "thou" and "thee" are a way in which Anne makes clear how she looks down on Gloucester with contempt. Thus, in *Othello* (I.i.118-19), Brabantio, aroused in the night to be told that his daughter has eloped, denounced Iago in these words: "Thou art a villain." To which Iago replies: "You are – a Senator."

In this contrived scene Richard's heartless cruelty and extreme egotism receive sufficient emphasis early and late. It is not stoicism primarily that explains his failure to shed a tear when Rutland and the Duke of York were slain, for he was already dedicated solely to the advancement of his own fortunes to the exclusion of any concern even for blood relatives. Near the end of the scene he callously refers to the corpse of Henry VI: "But first I'll turn yon fellow in his grave" – that is, he will toss or tip the body of his royal victim into the grave. He then tells the sun to shine so that he may see his shadow as it passes. Richard is saying that his physical deformity, symbol of his evil nature, is most pleasing to him, since it makes possible his advancement.

If the stress were placed solely upon Richard's monstrosity, upon the extreme violence of his actions, the villain-hero would not be the fascinating character that he is. Playing the role of a lover with consummate skill, he exhibits the daring, the superior wit, the profound sense of irony, the sheer intellectuality which mark him as one who indeed can outdo Machiavel. He is apparently unperturbed when Anne denounces him as a "dreadful minister of Hell" and as a "foul devil"; he seems to turn the other cheek and addresses her as a "Sweet saint" and gently reproves her for knowing "no rules of charity." Would even a ferocious beast know "some touch of pity" as Anne declares? Then, concludes the villain, he is not a beast! Once having conceded that he did kill Henry VI, Richard claims a kind of credit: he has helped the king to reach heaven. Essaying, for the nonce, the role of the Petrarchan lover, that swain whose avowals of undying love for his lady were recorded in the sonnet cycles already so popular in Shakespeare's England, Richard uses a typical conceit, or fanciful metaphor: he has been wounded to the quick by a glance of Anne's beautiful eyes.

But, like most of Shakespeare's villains, Richard can be completely honest with himself, as we learn from his soliloquies. That Anne, whose murdered husband is represented as having been a paragon of physical attractiveness and virtue, should have permitted this misshapen villain to win her so easily is, to Richard, most comically ironical. One other point, not to be ignored, is the irony in Anne's words when she exclaims: "Ill rest betide the chamber where thou liest" (112). In view of what we learn later, after Anne has been married to Richard for some time, this line is prophetic.

Finally, this scene reveals Richard's boundless energy. He has wasted no time in arranging the match with Lady Anne, as, at the end of the previous scene, we learned he planned to do.

ACT I–SCENE 3

Summary

At the palace, Queen Elizabeth is discussing with Lord Rivers, her brother, and Lord Grey, her son, the king's illness. Elizabeth is especially concerned with what her fate will be if her husband should die. As she points out to Lord Grey, her young son, the Prince of Wales, is "put unto the trust of Richard Gloucester," whom she knows to be her enemy and that of all the Woodville faction. The Duke of Buckingham and the Earl of Derby (also called Lord Stanley) enter and courteously greet the queen. To Derby she remarks that the Countess Richmond, his wife, would not say amen to his prayer for her happiness, for she is a woman of "proud arrogance" who does not cherish the queen. Derby insists that his wife is the victim of "false accusers"—either that or her attitude toward Elizabeth stems from perverse sickness, not malice. In response to a question, Buckingham reports that King Edward seems to have improved in health: he "speaks cheerfully" and is especially desirous of ending the quarrel between the queen's brothers and the offended Buckingham and Hastings. Elizabeth can only voice her fervent wish that all were well and to express the fear that her fortunes will not improve.

Richard, Hastings, and Lord Dorset (son to Elizabeth by her first marriage) enter. "They do me wrong, and I will not endure it." These are the first words of Richard, who presents himself as injured innocence, enraged because the queen's relatives have misrepresented him to the king. He offers himself as a simple, plain man, wronged by the insinuations of sly flatterers whom he cannot match because deception is no part of his character. When Rivers protests, Richard accuses him and all his family for troubling the king with vulgar complaints against him. Elizabeth explains that the king, seeing the hatred of the two families, merely wishes to find the cause of their ill will by having them meet with each other. Richard retorts surlily that he can no longer understand matters, now that the world is upside down, with every common fellow made a gentleman and every gentleman rudely treated like a common fellow.

The queen brings the quarrel into the open, saying that Gloucester envies the advancement of her family. Richard counters with the charge that the queen is responsible for Clarence's imprisonment. She protests. When Lord Rivers breaks in to defend her, Richard taunts her with having married a "handsome bachelor stripling," implying that she, an older widow, was not fit for one so young. The queen is stung by this and threatens to tell the king of all the insults she has borne from Richard.

Old Queen Margaret, widow of Henry VI, enters and stands apart, listening to the wrangling of her enemies, and now and then interjecting scathing comments on the words of successive speakers. To her it is a source of satisfaction that Elizabeth has small happiness in being Queen of England. Richard continues to speak to Elizabeth in his defense. Margaret interrupts him, calling him a devil and blaming him for the death of her husband and her son. Richard continues to address Elizabeth, ignoring the withering remarks of the aged Margaret. He states that, while Elizabeth and members of her family were on the side of the Lancastrians, he was the loyal Yorkist who helped Edward to the throne. Clarence, he continues, forsook his father-in-law Warwick, committing perjury in order to fight on Edward's side; for this offense he is now imprisoned. Interspersed between each of his statements are Margaret's denunciations, but Richard continues to ignore her. Lord Rivers argues that he and members of his family have been loyal always to their lawful king, as they would be to Richard, were he the ruler. Richard is quick to protest that he would rather be a beggar: "Far be it from my heart, the thought of it!" When this causes Elizabeth to bemoan her joyless lot once more, Margaret insists on being heard.

"Hear me, you wrangling pirates," she exclaims, and describes them as rebels who now are quarreling over that which they took from her. All who hear her join in reviling her for the indignity done to the Duke of York, whose severed head was fitted with a mock crown, and for the murder of his son Rutland. Margaret retaliates by asking whether all her sorrows and wrongs are not enough to justify that act of hers. Edward IV, Elizabeth, Rivers, Dorset, Hastings—all are the recipients of her curses as she calls upon God to punish her adversaries. Especially she curses Gloucester: may the "worm of conscience" afflict him; may only "deep traitors" be his friends; may he be deprived of restful sleep. She concludes by making much of his deformity as a sign that hell and the evil forces of nature have marked him for their own. Richard tries to turn the curses back on her. And when Elizabeth states that Margaret has indeed cursed herself, this "Poor painted [imitation] Queen," as she bitterly calls herself, concentrates her attack upon her royal successor and the Woodville faction in general, whom she identifies as upstarts. Ironically, Gloucester interposes an endorsement of her denunciation of Dorset and boasts that his own exalted status will prevent his fall. When Buckingham tries to restrain Margaret, she voices words of praise for him: since he had not fought against the Lancastrians, her curses do not apply to him. But Buckingham rejects her offer of "league and amity." It is then that Margaret warns him to beware of Richard upon whom "Sin, death, and Hell have set their marks." Finally she leaves.

Gloucester now sanctimoniously voices sympathy for Margaret and expresses regret for his part in having opposed her. When Elizabeth says that she is blameless, he points out that she has benefited by Margaret's downfall, whereas Richard himself had merely sought to help others. Again he makes reference to his brother Clarence, saying that Clarence suffers for the same reason and asking God to pardon those who are responsible for his brother's imprisonment. Lord Rivers sarcastically remarks on this "virtuous and Christianlike conclusion," but Richard remains unperturbed. His aside, however, makes it clear that, in praying for the forgiveness of any responsible for Clarence's fate, he avoided cursing himself.

Catesby enters and summons the group to the king's chambers. All except Richard leave, and in the final soliloquy he gloats over his villainy. He has furthered his ends by fooling Hastings, Derby, and Buckingham into believing that the queen's family is behind Clarence's ruin. When they try to persuade him to seek revenge, he puts on a saintly air and talks of returning good for evil. A fitting conclusion to this villainous speech is the entry of the two murderers whom he has hired to get rid of Clarence. They have come for the warrant which will provide for their admission to the Tower. He instructs them to feel no pity and not to be swayed by Clarence's eloquence. The first murderer assures Richard that they are doers, not talkers, and will carry out his instructions. They are instructed to go to Richard's home at Crosby Place after the deed is done.

Commentary

In the first scene, reference was made to the bitter quarrel between the members of the Woodville faction, headed by Queen Elizabeth, and high-ranking Yorkists, as well as such aristocrats as Lord Hastings, lord chamberlain to King Edward IV. Now the quarrel itself is dramatized, recrimination following recrimination. The extent of the dissension is indicated by the fact that the Countess Richmond, wife of Lord Stanley, Earl of Derby, detests Elizabeth as an upstart. It may be noted here that the countess is the mother of the Earl of Richmond, who will prove to be Richard's nemesis. But it is the Duke of Buckingham, in a sense an outsider as regards this quarrel, who clearly leans toward Gloucester, despite Queen Margaret's ominous warning. We may expect Richard to make the most of this turn of events.

A kind of suspense is achieved when Buckingham reports that the king's health seems to have improved and that Edward has moved to establish peace within his realm. Nothing is farther from Richard's wishes, to be sure; and he is relentless in his attack upon those who stand in his way. As the accomplished dissembler, he is no less effective than he was in the previous scene. Now he presents himself as the loyal, selfless subject of Edward IV opposed to those who are criminally ambitious — those whom he describes as "wrens" (the smallest of English birds) who "make prey where eagles dare not perch." The eagle, of course, is a symbol of royalty. Richard thus makes tacit reference to himself; and so when he confidently states that he is not one headed for catastrophe, since he was "born so high" (in contrast to the others present in this scene). Were not the Yorkists descended from Edward III? Once more Richard's feigned religiosity is apparent, as when he swears "By holy Paul" and "By God's holy mother." It is a good touch also to have him voice sympathy and Christian forgiveness for Queen Margaret, who has scathingly denounced him.

Especially important is the role of Queen Margaret, who makes her first appearance in this scene. As has been pointed out in the discussion of her character above, actually she had died in 1482. Even if she had survived, the appearance of this one-time champion of the house of Lancaster among her enemies is quite fantastic. Nevertheless, her role is a key one. Margaret immediately establishes herself as a terrifying chorus whose violent curses directed first to her successor, Queen Elizabeth, then repeatedly to Richard, and finally to Elizabeth's relatives, reveal her as a symbolic figure, "the doom of the House of York." At one point she denounces Richard as an "abortive, rooting hog." The reference is to his premature birth – evidence of his unnaturalness and perhaps the cause of his deformity – and to Richard's armorial crest, upon which was depicted a boar. The adjective "rooting" is meant to describe his destructive activities.

In this play, which has been called the most religious that Shakespeare ever wrote, it is Margaret who repeatedly emphasizes the major theme: God's inexorable justice visited upon those guilty of the heinous sins of murder and perjury. Richard is first to be charged with unforgivable crime – the murder of Henry VI and Edward, Prince of Wales. And when Gloucester, recalling that his brother Clarence had foresworn himself by deserting Warwick, hypocritically implores that Christ forgive the sinner, Margaret bitterly calls for God's vengeance upon Clarence. Once more it is a mathematical kind of justice – the logic of which so appealed to Elizabethans – that she emphasizes when she summarizes her indictment of those responsible for the fall of the house of Lancaster. Her speech begins with these words addressed to Elizabeth:

> For Edward thy son, which now is Prince of Wales
> For Edward my son, which was Prince of Wales.
>
> (200-201)

It ends with her fervent prayer:

> That none of you may live your natural age.
> But by some unlooked accident cut off!
>
> (213-14)

In the course of the subsequent action, vengeance will indeed be visited upon each of those whom Margaret indicts.

But what of this aged former queen who has suffered and is suffering so much? Richard reminds her of her own offenses – how she had deserved the Duke of York's curses and how the young Duke of Rutland had been killed by the Lancastrians. Familiar as they were with the history of these times, members of Shakespeare's audiences would not fail to recall that Henry VI, although widely praised for his piety, was the grandson of a regicide and usurper, one who had seized the throne from the lawful, anointed King Richard II, from which deed all these troubles had stemmed. Did not the Bible say that the crimes of the father would be visited upon the children even unto the third generation?

Summary

The action now takes place in the Tower of London, toward which, as we learned at the end of scene iii, the murderers repair. The imprisoned Clarence tells Brakenbury, the Lieutenant of the Tower and therefore his jailer, about the miserable night he has endured. He explains that he thought that he was on a ship bound for Burgundy when his brother Gloucester induced him to come and walk the deck. As they talked of their adventures during the recent wars, Richard stumbled and, when Clarence tried to help him, Clarence himself was struck by his brother and fell overboard. The royal prisoner then gives a most vivid description of his dream of drowning, which was continued to the point where his soul was being ferried over the "melancholy flood" of the River Styx by the ferryman Charon. There he met Warwick, whom he had betrayed, followed by the ghost of Prince Edward, whom he had stabbed at Tewkesbury. Clarence hears himself described as "false, fleeting, perjured Clarence." Convinced that he was in hell, Clarence remembers all the deeds which might have sent him there. He prays God to punish him if He must, but to spare his wife and children.

As Clarence sleeps, Brakenbury, moved by the recital, reflects on the sorrow of princes who, despite their high rank, often feel "a world of restless care," as do lesser folk. He is interrupted by the two murderers. They show their warrants and are left in charge of the sleeping prince, while the lieutenant goes back to the king to resign his commission.

The murderers discuss killing Clarence while he sleeps, but the mention of "judgment" arouses the conscience of the second murderer. It is the fear that he will face damnation despite the warrant to perform the deed received from Richard. In contrast, the first murderer is obviously one who will dare damnation to earn the promised monetary reward. At the mention of that reward, the second murderer finds that his conscience no longer is an impediment. As the two are talking about the inconveniences of conscience and holding a kind of dialogue between conscience and the devil, they finally decide to strike Clarence over the head and then drop him into a butt of malmsey wine. Clarence awakes and calls for a cup of wine. Grimly ironical, the first murderer replies: "You shall have wine enough, my lord, anon" – that is, immediately.

In the colloquy that follows, Clarence learns that these are his executioners, and is first led to believe that they have been sent on the orders of King Edward to put to death one guilty of treason. He is eloquent in his own defense and attempts to dissuade the murderers, but they remain adamant. They remind him of his heinous crimes of perjury and murder, for (we now learn) he had joined his brother Richard in killing Prince Edward. Clarence declares that he had acted solely on behalf of his brother Edward, who therefore is quite as deep in sin as is Clarence himself. In this exchange, the royal prisoner refers repeatedly to his brother, meaning Edward, but soon learns, to his utter dismay, that the determined first murderer uses the term to refer to Gloucester. Again Clarence invokes God's name, urging his adversaries to relent. And again the second murderer wavers, even warning Clarence that the first murderer is about to strike him. But it is too late. Clarence is stabbed several times, and his murderer leaves with the duke's body, which he will throw into the "malmsey butt within." Now the second murderer is indeed conscience-stricken. The scene ends with the actual murderer accusing the accessory of cowardice and threatening to denounce him to Richard.

Commentary

This is a highly dramatic scene which contains much that is doctrinally and thematically important. Clarence's long speeches addressed to Braken-bury follow the tradition established by that popular collection of tragical histories in verse entitled *Mirror for Magistrates,* a work of accretion, the first edition of which appeared in 1559. Other editions followed in 1571, 1574, 1575, 1578, and 1587. (Cf. Lily B. Campell, *Shakespeare's Histories: Mirrors of Elizabethan Policy,* San Marino, California, 1947, Chap. XVI.) Significant is the fact that the *Mirror* dealt primarily with English history from the reign of Richard II to the fall of Richard III at Bosworth's Field in 1485. It mirrors the instability of fortune and the punishment of vice, and, as we are told in one of the prose introductions, seeks "by example of other's miseries to dissuade all men from sins and vices." Successively the ghosts of fallen great persons tell their stories in long monologues, announcing their own guilt and usually stressing the theme of divine vengeance. In the development of this theme in Shakespeare's play, the supernatural, includ-ing portentous dreams, has an important place. In Clarence's terrifying dream appears the ghost of Warwick to denounce him as "false, fleeting, perjured Clarence."

Clarence's first long speech (9-33) is, of its kind, quite superior as poetry. If indeed Shakespeare still writes a predominantly Marlovian type of verse, the lines of which are usually end-stopped, he incorporates spe-cific details in a way hardly characteristic of Marlowe, so that every line evokes a picture. Notable is the way in which the poet builds up to cli-maxes: "All scattered in the bottom of the sea" (28) and "And mocked the dead bones that lay scattered by" (33). Following each the rhythm of Clarence's lines changes appropriately.

The second long speech (43-63) contains Clarence's outburst of self-incrimination, leaving no doubt of his particular guilt. But he remains a human being and invites our sympathy. Unselfishly he thinks of his family and courageously he meets his violent death. Nevertheless, one must not lose sight of the fact that he is a grievous sinner who must endure the inevitable punishment of a just God in accordance with the orthodox doctrine which informs this play.

The two murderers are exceptionally well individualized. Their prose dialogue is most realistic and packed with grim humor. Note, for example, the second murderer's speech in which he indicts conscience on the grounds that "it makes a man a coward" (137-48). When asked scornfully if he is afraid, he replies: "Not to kill him, having a warrant for it, but to be damned for killing him, from which no warrant can defend us" (112-14).

The question is one regarding vengeance in general. The proper authority, functioning as God's minister on earth, as he is called in Romans 13, can and must execute public justice; but no one, however exalted his position, can rightfully execute private revenge. This is the import of Clarence's argument as he seeks to dissuade the murderer:

> Erroneous vassal! The great King of Kings
> Hath in his tables of His law commanded
> That thou shalt do no murder. And wilt thou then
> Spurn His edict, and fulfill a man's?
> Take heed, for He holds vengeance in His hands,
> To hurl upon the heads that break his law.
>
> (200-205)

The second murderer, to whom these lines were addressed, has an answer:

> And that same vengeance doth He hurl on thee,
> For false swearing, and for murder too.
>
> (206-07)

Clarence argues that these crimes were committed for Edward's sake, and that the king is therefore quite as deep in sin as is Clarence himself. He goes on:

> If God will be revenged for this deed,
> Oh, know you yet, He doth it publicly.   (221-22)

—that is, the king will observe the due process of law.

And then the doomed Clarence learns that these murderers serve his brother Gloucester, whose motive is criminal ambition, not revenge, public or private. What conclusions are to be drawn from all this? There is no doubt that Clarence deserved extreme punishment. But how to account for the fact that two murderers hired by an arch-villain perform the deed? Is this an example of God's inexorable justice? According to Tudor theory it was exactly that. Just as God may permit the rebel to rage in order to punish a sinful ruler, so may He use even such sinners as Richard and, at a different level, the hired assassins, to execute his justice against Clarence. They function as the Scourge of God. But, still in keeping with the larger concept of justice, they will be scourged in turn ultimately. In the previous scene Margaret had implored God to punish Clarence: her prayer has been answered. At the end of this scene, the second murderer acknowledges the fact that the two have "most grievous murder done," and he will have no share in the promised reward, the thought of which earlier had led him to spurn the urgings of conscience. There is, then, no contradiction, no inconsistency, here in the sustaining of the play's major theme.

ACT II – SCENE 1

Summary

The scene shifts to the palace. King Edward, whom we meet for the first time, has called the queen and members of the family and court to his bedside. He commands them to be reconciled to one another and to swear to refrain from enmity in the future. Successively Rivers, Hastings, the queen herself, Dorset, Buckingham solemnly take the sacred vow. Only Gloucester is absent "To make the perfect period of this peace," to use the king's words. But Richard makes his appearance immediately, wishing all present "a happy time of day." When he is told that all differences have been settled and that hate has now given place to "fair love," he pronounces the king's action to be "a blessed labor" and, insisting that he desires "all good men's love," declares himself to be devoted to all present. He concludes by piously thanking God for his humility.

When Queen Elizabeth, anxious that the new-found amity be extended to all members of the court group, urges the king to pardon Clarence,

Richard delivers the shocking news that Clarence is dead: Edward's reprieve had arrived too late. Almost at once Derby enters and begs that his servent's life, declared forfeit for murder, be spared. This request fills Edward with remorse as he contrasts the zeal of a master for a servant with the neglect of Clarence. Especially he remembers all that Clarence had done for him, and he blames not only himself but all others present, none of whom had interceded in Clarence's behalf. Edward concludes that he and the rest have rendered themselves subject to God's punishment. Calling Hastings, the lord chamberlain, to accompany him, he leaves with the queen and some members of the court.

Gloucester promptly takes advantage of the occasion to draw Buckingham's attention to what he describes as the guilty looks of the queen's relatives. He charges that they had urged the king to put Clarence to death, and he predicts that "God will avenge it." He then asks Buckingham to join him in comforting Edward.

Commentary

Conflict is, of course, the essence of drama. In Act I Richard emerged ahead in his conflict with a society, indeed with the state itself. Now events occur which suggest that the odds have shifted. The ailing king appears to have quieted the quarreling factions, as the first two lines of the scene make clear. This is a solemn occasion for all concerned, for England's king is on his deathbed. As Tudor political philosophy had it, the subject, whatever his rank, is to the ruler as is the child to his parent. Vows made to a king are especially sacred, thus the import of Edward's admonition beginning "Take heed you dally not before your King" (13-15). Note that both Rivers and Hastings are vehement in their avowals, and so the rest. But most eloquent is Buckingham, who had been held blameless by the rapacious Queen Margaret. Each has committed himself irrevocably, inviting God's punishment if the oath is violated.

The ethical significance of Clarence's death is now made crystal clear: inexorable justice is operating once more. Practically all of the characters in this scene deserve or will deserve divine punishment. And in this connection, note that the last two lines of King Edward's long reply to Derby are portentous:

> O God, I fear Thy justice will take hold
> On me and you, and mine and yours for this!

How ironical are Richard's words addressed to Buckingham, spoken as they are by the one who is directly responsible for Clarence's death: "God will revenge it" (138).

Score another point for the villain-hero, that master dissembler who had intercepted the orders countermanding the execution of Clarence. So far from amity flourishing, the split is greater than before. The immediate point is that God's justice continues to be administered and Richard continues to function as His scourge. Significantly, it is Buckingham who has the final line. If we had any doubts heretofore, we now know that he has committed himself to serve Richard for his own purposes.

ACT II – SCENE 2

Summary

In a mood consistent with Edward's remorse and sorrow, this scene introduces the young son and daughter of Clarence, who suspect that their father is dead. They are talking to their grandmother, the Duchess of York, who is weeping not, as they think, for Clarence but for the mortally sick king. Richard has succeeded in convincing these children that Edward, influenced by Queen Elizabeth, is responsible for their father's death. He has assured them of his devotion to them and has told them to rely on him. Richard's mother, fully aware of her son's intent, laments that she has given birth to so foul a monster. But Clarence's young son finds it impossible to believe that his uncle could be such a villain.

Queen Elizabeth, grief-stricken and all disheveled, enters. All now learn that King Edward is dead, and a general chorus of grief ensues. The duchess weeps for her husband and two sons, the queen for her husband, and the children for their father. Dorset and Rivers try to comfort the queen, Rivers immediately introducing the comforting thought of her son, who should be summoned from Ludlow immediately to be crowned.

Gloucester comes in with Buckingham, Derby, Hastings, and Ratcliff. He is in good form as usual, offering words of comfort to Queen Elizabeth and asking his mother's blessing. Buckingham suggests that the Prince of Wales be brought from Ludlow with a small group of followers and succeeds in convincing Rivers that a larger group might lead to a new outbreak of trouble. All the while, Richard presents himself as one only too ready to cooperate in carrying out the will of the others. All except Buckingham and Gloucester retire to discuss the proposal. The exchange between the two makes clear the fact that Richard has been letting Buckingham play the man of action and do the talking and that there is an arrangement for them "to part the Queen's proud kindred from the king." They set forth for Ludlow.

Commentary

The first part of this scene serves to point up the tragedy that has befallen the house of York. There is much that is formally ritualistic here, and the pronounced religious tone is evident enough. Thus one of Clarence's children, having been led to believe that King Edward was directly responsible for his father's death, says:

> God will avenge it, Whom I will importune
> With daily prayer to that effect.   (14-15)

And Dorset, seeking to comfort his bereaved mother, Elizabeth, voices the orthodox views on Christian forbearance in the passage beginning "God is displeased That you take with unthankfulness His doing" (89-95). In this way, the major theme is kept to the fore.

To some it may seem that the Duchess of York takes a rather heartless attitude toward the death of Clarence when she explains that she laments "the sickness of the King," not the loss of her other son: "It were lost sorrow to wail one that's lost" (11). But this is consistent with Christian teaching, certainly with that which flourished in Shakespeare's England. Elsewhere in Shakespeare, one finds expression of the idea that life is a loan from God to be repaid when He demands it, and Dorset's speech addressed to Elizabeth repeats this idea. Undue grief for the dead was thought to imply a question of God's dealings with mortals. Moreover, Edward is not only the duchess's son; he is the king, and she is one of his subjects. What happens to Edward is a matter of public concern; the welfare of the state is involved. And, of course, all this adds to the religious tone.

Queen Elizabeth, "with her hair about her ears," is the very symbol of tormented grief. Her first speech provides a good example of the highly mannered, rhetorical style to which reference was made in the critical introduction above. This is typical of early Shakespeare, reflecting the influence of Seneca—at least the Seneca of the popular stage. In this connection, note the sentential elements in her speech, as when she exclaims:

> Why grow the branches now the root is withered?
> Why wither not the leaves, the sap being gone?   (41-42)

36

Senecan also is the exchange between the children and the two queen-mothers beginning "Oh, for our father, for our dear lord Clarence!" (72-79) These lines provide an example of *stichomythia,* which has been defined in the introduction.

Edward did not die a violent death, as did Clarence. Nevertheless, his death is part of the larger pattern: the grievous sinner cannot escape God's justice.

While tracing the dominant theme in *Richard III,* we must not ignore the skill with which Shakespeare delineates the character of Gloucester, who early and late holds the interest of all readers and members of an audience, whether or not they be interested in or concerned about the major theme of the play. Consistently this Machiavellian villain who rejects God gives us a good example of his cynical humor in his aside after his mother complies with his expressed wish that she give him her blessing.

The action continues to rise and an element of suspense is introduced in this scene. Rivers urges Queen Elizabeth to see to it that her son be crowned as soon as possible. Obviously, the coronation would be a great setback for the ambitious Richard, and might make it impossible for him to advance his evil fortunes. But Richard is never to be underestimated. He has taken steps to forestall the coronation and to remove the prince from the protection and influence of the queen's family. And Gloucester, who more than once has made reference to his simplicity and humility, grossly flatters his dupe, Buckingham, speaking of himself as a child willingly guided by this "oracle" and "prophet." At his level, let it be remembered, Buckingham is no less selfishly ambitious than Richard.

ACT II – SCENE 3

Summary

Three London citizens meet in a street and discuss the news of the king's death. Each has a clearly marked character. The first citizen is optimistic, almost buoyantly so. The second citizen is not so confident as he voices the traditional fear that change, particularly in matters relating to the state, are not usually for the better. He places his hope in the conviction that Edward IV's young son will be guided wisely by his counselors. The third citizen, however, is a thoroughgoing pessimist. He predicts "a troublesome world," especially because the new king is "in his nonage," that is, his boyhood. When Henry VI, then a mere child, came to the throne, virtuous uncles were at hand to give him prudent counsel. Not so now, for "full of danger is the Duke of Gloucester," and "the Queen's kindred [are] haughty and proud." In a series of sententious lines, he concludes that it is wise to fear the worst. All three, instructed to appear before the justices, depart together.

Commentary

This short scene allows for the necessary passage of time for the arrests of which we learn in the next scene. But its chief importance is to emphasize the fact that (as in all Shakespeare's chronicle history plays) the state is the real protagonist in the larger sense; for it is the welfare of England, the well-being of all subjects, that is of first importance. When the sententious third citizen exclaims "Woe to that land that's governed by a child," he is para-phrasing Ecclesiastes 10:16 ("Woe to thee, O land, when thy king is a child..."). The text is voiced twice by Buckingham in Edward Hall's chronicle history of these events (1548) and had long since become proverbial. Note that the third citizen expresses the conviction that, if England is to suffer as a result of Edward IV's death, it deserves to suffer, since all things are in God's hands (36-37). This constant reference to God is a tacit reminder that His justice always is operative, whatever the conditions may be, and particularly so with reference to the state. The "virtuous uncles" of Henry VI (21) were the Dukes of Bedford and Gloucester, who prosecuted the war against France. The commoners of England, it is clear, are aware of the bitter rivalries at court, rivalries which may lead to violence and destruction at this time of the succession. And they can only voice their hopes and fears and remain passively obedient.

ACT II–SCENE 4

Summary

The archbishop announces that the party bringing the young prince will arrive within a day or so. This begins a conversation about the appearance of the prince, whom the mother, grandmother, and younger brother are anxious to see. The queen hopes that he has grown; his grandmother has heard, however, that the nine-year-old duke has almost overtaken him. The boy hopes this is not so, for his uncle Gloucester has told him that "small herbs have grace, great weeds grow apace." The old duchess retorts that, since Richard grew slowly, if this were so he should be full of grace, about which she ironically expresses her doubts. The precocious boy remembers a story he has heard that Richard was born with all his teeth, and must have grown fast, since he could "gnaw a crust at two hours old." A biting jest indeed for a boy of nine! Since getting teeth early was also believed to be a sign of villainous disposition, the two women recognize the boy's shrewdness, and his mother rebukes him for being mischievous.

38

Dorset enters with the upsetting news that Lord Rivers, Lord Grey, and Sir Thomas Vaughan have all been sent to Pomfret Castle, imprisoned by the "mighty dukes," Gloucester and Buckingham. Dorset does not know what accusation had been brought against them. The queen, rightly seeing the downfall of her house, bemoans the tyranny that preys on the young king's innocence. The Duchess of York cries out against yet another indication of the dreadful war of blood against blood and self against self for the crown. The queen takes the boy to sanctuary, led by the Archbishop of York, who gives the Great Seal into her keeping.

Commentary

The young Duke of York's instinctive dislike and distrust of his uncle is a prelude to the news that Gloucester has struck his first blow against the princes. Having seen to it that the queen's son and brother, as well as Sir Thomas Vaughan, constant and faithful attendant on young Edward from the new king's infancy, are imprisoned in Pomfret Castle, Richard now has all active power in his hands. That Pomfret should be the place of imprisonment is in itself especially ominous, for there Richard II and many others had met their deaths.

This scene derives, at least ultimately, from More's account, in which it is stated that the archbishop had been roused "not long after midnight" by a messenger from Lord Hastings, who had reported that Gloucester and Buckingham had taken young Edward V, then on his way to London, from Stony Stratford back twelve miles to Northampton. It has been argued that "if the Archbishop knew that the young king had been carried back to Northampton, he must also have known that the lords who accompanied him were sent to prison." Long since it has been pointed out, however, that "Shakespeare deviates a little from historical truth in order to attain dramatic effect: he makes the messenger arrive *during* the archbishop's interview with the queen, whereas, actually, it was the news that the messenger brought that led to the interview" (*Variorum*, p. 184). As Shakespeare dramatizes the event, one must assume that the news of the return to Northampton made the archbishop so apprehensive that he hurried to the queen bearing the Great Seal, without which the highest acts of state could not be ratified formally.

ACT III – SCENE 1

Summary

A flourish of trumpets announces the arrival of the young prince, followed by Gloucester and Buckingham, Cardinal Bourchier, Catesby, and others. From the first the prince is melancholy. He wants (that is, lacks) "more uncles" to welcome him and is not convinced when Richard implies that they were false friends from whom he is better protected. The lord mayor, appropriately attended, enters and greets the uncrowned king. The youth responds courteously and then again complains about not seeing his mother and brother.

As the prince further complains about the absence of Hastings, that lord enters with the news that the queen has taken the young Duke of York into sanctuary, he knows not why. Buckingham tells Cardinal Bourchier to fetch the boy by force if necessary, but that dignitary objects to violating the "holy privilege." Buckingham overcomes the objections by reasoning that the law of sanctuary is not valid in such a "gross" age and that the boy is too young and innocent to need or ask for sanctuary in any case. The cardinal is easily convinced, and he sets out, accompanied by Hastings.

The prince asks his uncle where he will stay until the coronation. Richard advises him to resort to the Tower, the thought of which does not appeal to the prince. Since Julius Caesar was then credited with having built the Tower of London, the prince and Gloucester engage in a dialogue concerning Julius Caesar and the nature of reputation and fame.

Hastings and the cardinal return, bringing with them the young Duke of York, who, after greeting his brother and referring to his father's death, quickly takes the opportunity to flout his uncle. He refers to his own growth, trying to make Richard repeat the compromising speech about the young king's idleness referred to in the previous scene. He next begs a dagger from his uncle and jests about the possibility of Richard's giving him his sword. This sharp speech culminates in the boy's joking allusion to his uncle's crooked shoulders. Buckingham expresses admiration for the young duke's precosity, but Richard apparently ignores it. He urges Edward and his brother to leave for the Tower. Meanwhile, he will entreat Elizabeth, the queen-mother, to join them there. The duke demurs, saying that he will not sleep quiet in the place where his uncle Clarence had been murdered. Edward, however, says that he fears no uncles dead. And to Gloucester's "nor none that live, I hope," he retorts "and if they live, I hope I need not fear." His thoughts, obviously, are about Lord Rivers. The children go unhappily to the Tower.

Buckingham again comments on the wit of the young duke, suggesting that he may have been incited by his mother to taunt Richard. Richard's reply, "No doubt...he is all his mother's," brings out at once the contrast between the two children and Gloucester's deep hatred of the queen-mother and her faction. Buckingham calls Catesby over and takes the initiative in sounding him out as to the possibilities of winning Hastings over to their side. Catesby suggests that Hasting's great loyalty to Edward IV will keep him from doing anything against the prince, and that Stanley will do whatever Hastings does. Buckingham sends him off to sound out Hastings and summon him to the Tower to join the counsel in discussing the coronation. It is Richard who gives Catesby the final order: "Shall we hear from you, Catesby, ere we sleep?"

After Catesby has left, Buckingham wonders what will be done with Hastings if he proves unwilling to go along with their plots. As if there were no possible question, Richard says, "Chop off his head," and reminds Buckingham to ask for the earldom of Hereford and related properties when Richard becomes king. Buckingham replies that he will indeed claim the promised reward, and the two retire to sup and arrange their plans.

Commentary

In this scene we witness the always energetic Gloucester preparing for the removal of obstacles in his quest for the crown. The chief obstacles are, of course, the uncrowned boy, King Edward, and his brother, the Duke of York. But there are also Lords Stanley and Hastings to be considered, and they must be dealt with. Richard is nothing if not the capable executive. He leaves to the well-schooled Buckingham the task of making suggestions and arguments so that Richard himself usually appears as one seeking to be helpful and cooperative. Buckingham provides an interesting contrast to Catesby, who also serves Richard. Catesby awaits only instruction to carry out an order without question; he requires no special handling. But Buckingham is vain of his talents and responds readily to Gloucester's flattery, as when he is called "my thought's sovereignty" — i.e., king of my thoughts (2). He possesses considerable political ability and the powers of subtle contrivance. Sophistry characterizes his words to young Edward beginning "Sweet Prince, the untainted virtue of your years/ Hath not yet dived into the world's deceit" (7-15) and his reply to the cardinal, whom he finds to be "too senseless obstinate,/ Too ceremonial and traditional" (44-56). In pursuit of his own goal, he is not troubled much by conscience. When Richard informs him that, if Hastings does not prove pliable his head must be chopped off, Buckingham thinks only of the promised reward: the earldom of Hereford, together with all "movables" (goods) which had been confiscated by King Edward IV.

Of interest also are the contrasting characters of the two royal brothers. Edward is grave, thoughtful, conscious already of his responsibilities; thus his rebuke to the Duke of York: "A beggar, brother?" (112) The ironic dialogue about Julius Caesar and the nature of fame leads him to express his own ambition to win renown: "I'll win our ancient right in France again ..." (92). The implication is that, if he be permitted to survive and to rule England, internecine conflict would no longer occur; rather, the ruler would win fame in fighting a foreign enemy. In the polemical literature of the age, the horrors of civil war were frequently contrasted with the glory to be won in a conflict legitimately waged against the country's foe. Tacitly suggested also is that Edward's villainous uncle will achieve not fame but infamy in the annals of history.

The Duke of York is a "parlous boy" (154), that is, dangerously cunning from the points of view of Buckingham and Richard. He is "bold, quick, ingenious, forward, capable [intelligent]." Like his royal brother he is deeply suspicious of his uncle Gloucester. Indeed, his instinctive dislike and distrust, established in the previous scene, is emphasized here. When he asks for his uncle's dagger, he means much more than that involved in a natural request made by a pert, forward lad; he intimates that Gloucester should be rendered harmless by being disarmed. Farther along in the dialogue he wittily alludes to Richard's deformity and tacitly calls him a fool. This is introduced with the play upon the word *bear* (127). "Because I am little, like an ape/ He thinks that you should bear me on your shoulders" (130-31). In Buckingham's words, "With what sharp-provided wit he reasons!"

In this scene, Shakespeare arouses the tragic emotions of pity and fear for the boy king and his brother. He does so particularly by means of the double meanings typically found in Richard's discourse, as when he says "A greater gift I'll give my cousin" (115), and in his ominous asides: "So wise so young, they say, do not live long" (79) and "Short summers lightly have a forward spring" (94). Furthermore, established here are the probable positions of Hastings and Stanley.

The doctrinal element is not absent from this scene. That Buckingham, actually the voice of Richard, should reject the concept of sanctuary as a "holy privilege" and that Edward V is not to Richard a "dread sovereign" underscores the fact that the sins involved are sins against religion, against God — sins which invite His inexorable justice. For in accordance with politico-religious thinking in the Age of Elizabeth, the sovereign was indeed to be dreaded — to be held in awe or "feared" in the Biblical sense. Again let it be remembered that the ruler was accepted as God's lieutenant on earth by the orthodox.

ACT III – SCENE 2

Summary

The scene begins with the arrival of a messenger at Lord Hasting's house at four o'clock in the morning. The messenger comes from Lord Stanley, who has had a premonitory dream about "the boar" which destroyed his helmet. Stanley is so disturbed that he wishes Hastings to flee with him to the north. Hastings scorns the advice and sends the messenger back. He knows of the two councils which are to be held; but since he will be in one and his servant Catesby in the other, there can be nothing to fear. Moreover,

> To fly the boar before the boar pursues
> Were to incense the boar to follow us,
> And make pursuit where he did mean no chase. (28-30)

Stanley is instead to rise and go with him to the Tower. As the messenger leaves, Catesby enters and cunningly tests Hastings' loyalty by saying that things will never be right in the kingdom until Richard wears the crown. Hastings remains loyal to the young prince and does not waver in his devotion even when told that his enemies, members of the queen's family, have been put to death at Pomfret. Not even if his life were at stake would Hastings move to prevent the "true descent" of Edward IV's heirs. The wary Catesby, his mission accomplished, sanctimoniously approves Hastings' declaration of loyalty: "God keep your lordship in that gracious mind!" (56)

The confident Hastings now begins to boast of those he will get rid of within a fortnight, relying as he does on the favor of Richard and Buckingham. Catesby encourages this opinion, but his aside makes clear that Hastings has, as it were, pronounced sentence upon himself and that Richard and Buckingham will see to it that Hastings is put to death as a traitor.

Stanley appears, still uneasy, and Hastings reasserts his buoyant confidence. Stanley reminds him that the lords imprisoned at Pomfret had been no less sure of themselves. When he is told that those lords are to be beheaded, he again voices his fears, suggesting that those who are to die may be better men than some who have brought charges against them. When Catesby and Stanley leave, Hastings continues to express his complete confidence in an exchange with a pursuivant whom he had met earlier when on his way to be imprisoned in the Tower. A priest enters and greets him. Hastings thanks him, acknowledges indebtedness for the priest's service, and promises to reward him on the next Sabbath. Buckingham enters and remarks that, unlike his friends at Pomfret, Hastings has no need for a priest

—that is, no urgent need for confession and absolution. Hastings replies that the thoughts of Rivers, Vaughan, and Grey had indeed come to his mind as he talked with the priest. He then asks whether Buckingham is going to the Tower. The latter's reply is sinister enough, although Hastings is unaware of the fact:

> I do, my lord, but long I shall not stay.
> I shall return before your lordship thence.   (120-21)

Commentary

In *Romeo and Juliet,* the romantic tragedy which dates some two years later than *Richard III,* Shakespeare assigns these lines to Romeo near the end of the play:

> How oft when men are at the point of death
> Have they been merry! Which their keepers call
> A lightening before death.   (V.iii.88-90)

"A lightening before death"—that is the theme of this scene in which Hastings is the chief character. He remains merry and confident, unperturbed by the report of Stanley's ominous dream of the boar that razed the helmet. Since Gloucester's crest is the boar, the interpretation of this dream poses no problem: those who stand in Richard's way invite death.

Shakespeare follows Holinshed in identifying Catesby as one of Hastings' servingmen. But already we have learned that Catesby had become dedicated to Richard, whose most recent orders he is now carrying out. As far as Hastings is concerned, the concept of tragedy in this scene is medieval. He is at the top of Fortune's Wheel, supremely confident of his own well-being and future. Stanley's dream, the ironical comments and the aside of Catesby, the appearance of the priest, and Buckingham's sinister remarks—all are either ignored or misunderstood by Hastings. But they indicate that Fortune's Wheel is about to turn once more. He seems to invite disaster when he gloats over the thought of the impending executions of Rivers, Vaughan, and Grey, as well as to predict the downfall of others. Nevertheless, in his unshakable loyalty to Edward IV and to Edward's heir, he appears to be an exemplum of righteousness. By implication, at least, Catesby acknowledges as much when he says: "God keep your lordship in that gracious [holy] mind." Catesby, who is in the process of violating his trust to his master, is not moved by such graciousness. Then why, one may ask, should Hastings be marked for death? The answer is that, as an active adherent to the Yorkist cause he also is guilty. Recall that Queen Margaret had identified him as one of the "standers-by" when her son had been "stabbed with bloody daggers" (I.iii.210-12). All this, there-fore, is part of the fulfillment of the curse upon the house of York.

ACT III – SCENE 3

Summary

This scene at Pomfret Castle concludes the story of the queen's rela-tives. Ratcliff, one of Richard's henchmen, enters leading Rivers, Grey, and Vaughan to death. Rivers protests that he is dying "For truth, for duty, and for loyalty." Grey thinks of the prince and prays that he may be kept safe from this pack of bloodsuckers. As Ratcliff hurries them Rivers speaks again, remembering that Pomfret was the scene of Richard II's murder. Grey thinks of Margaret's curse, and Rivers recalls that she cursed Has-tings, Buckingham, and Richard also. He prays in one breath that those curses will be fulfilled, and in the next asks God to consider the blood about to be shed enough to save Elizabeth and the prince. Again enjoined by Ratcliff to hurry, they embrace each other and leave to meet their doom.

Commentary

The careful reader may be surprised to find Ratcliff at Pomfret, which is in Yorkshire, since he appears at the Tower of London in the next scene. Obviously Shakespeare trusted to the imagination of his audience rather than to their geographical knowledge. This, to be sure, is a minor point. There are two major ones to be made. First, it is again made clear that the dethronement and murder of Richard II, a lawful, anointed king, started all these bloody events; for that was the prime action which invited vengeance upon the guilty members of the houses of Lancaster and York. Second, Gloucester, arch-villain though he is, continues to be the immediate instrument of divine justice. Grey acknowledges his own guilt and that of Rivers and Vaughan: all three had been accessories to the murder of Queen Margaret's son.

ACT III – SCENE 4

Summary

This is the meeting at the Tower to which Hastings and Stanley have been summoned to discuss the date of the coronation. The Bishop of Ely suggests the following day, but as Richard is not yet present they hesitate to decide without him. Cunningly, Buckingham asks who is most intimate with Richard. To the bishop's reply that he himself is, Buckingham an-swers ironically that, unlike faces, hearts remain unrevealed. He then calls upon Hastings, who, confident that he stands high in Gloucester's affec-tions, offers to speak for him. At that very moment Gloucester enters, and Buckingham is careful to let him know what Hastings had said.

For no apparent reason other than unusually high spirits, Richard begs the bishop to send for some fine strawberries Richard had seen in his garden. When the bishop leaves, Richard calls Buckingham aside to report that Hastings will never consent to oppose the coronation of the prince. The two leave the stage. Lord Stanley (called Derby in this scene) expresses the opinion that the coronation should be postponed until the next day. The bishop returns, looking about for Richard, and Hastings remarks that Gloucester "looks most cheerfully and smooth"; he is sure that Richard's face reveals the heart of a man who is offended with no one. As Stanley, still uneasy, prays that this is true, Gloucester and Buckingham return.

Richard's mood has changed completely. He demands to know what should be done with those who have planned his death by means of witchcraft. Hastings has the answer: they should be put to death. Drawing back his sleeve to show his withered arm, Richard blames the queen and Mistress Shore. "If they have done this, my gracious Lord—." So Hastings begins. He is not allowed to finish. Gloucester seized upon the conditional *If* and denounces him as the "protector of this damned strumpet," Jane Shore. Hastings further hears himself declared to be a traitor and sentenced to death. Lovel and Ratcliff are ordered to carry out the sentence.

Only Hastings and his executioners remain onstage. In his dying speech Hastings laments the fate of England and regrets his own foolish confidence, his ignoring of ominous portents. Even his horse, clad in ceremonial dress and proceeding at a walking pace, had stumbled three times on its way to the Tower, as if unwilling to carry its master to his death. He remembers the priest, whom he now needs for himself, and the pursuivant who had listened to him gloat over the impending deaths of Rivers, Vaughan, and Grey. He remembers also Queen Margaret's curse.

Catesby abruptly orders him to hurry in order not to delay Gloucester's dinner. Lovel rudely interrupts his final musings on the vanity of man and the shortness of life. Prophesying "the fearfulls't time" for England and the same fate as his for those who smile at him today, Hastings is led off to the block.

Commentary

Buckingham's reply to the Bishop of Ely's questions ("Who knows the Lord Protector's mind herein? Who is most inward with the noble Duke?") sums up the whole extent of Buckingham's deception of others and of Richard's deception of him. It is, then, a prime example of irony in a scene packed with irony.

Richard's superior cunning, no less than his heartlessness, again is dramatized here. With what skill he first presents himself plausibly as the man of good will. "I have been a sleeper," he explains to the "noble lords and cousins" assembled in the Tower (24). Richard a sleeper — he who continues to reveal himself as the most energetic character in the play! The apparently irrelevant bit relating to the strawberries in the bishop's garden, the details of which appear in More's account and in Holinshed, serves Shakespeare's purpose in this connection, for it shows Richard displaying affability and good humor, a careless ease in the midst of his crimes. Little wonder that Lord Hastings should be deceived completely. Hazlitt (*Characters of Shakespeare's Plays*, 1817-18, p. 153) found Hastings' belief that "with no man here he [Richard] is offended" (58) to be one of the "finest strokes in the play," showing as it does "the deep, plausible manners of Richard." One conclusion to be drawn is that Hastings is not to be dismissed as incredibly naive, even if he is not wary as is Stanley. He is one of those individuals who, to borrow a line from another Shakespearean play, "believe men honest who but seem so." In no circumstance must one underestimate Gloucester's skill as a dissembler.

After Edward IV's death, Jane Shore had become Hastings' mistress. It will be recalled that Richard had told Catesby to inform Hastings that his "dangerous adversaries" were to be executed and to bid him "give Mistress Shore one gentle kiss the more" (III.i.185). The attractive daughter of a London goldsmith had indeed been accused of witchcraft, and Hastings' relations with her therefore worked to Richard's advantage. Shakespeare's audiences would not have considered the accusation to be absurd. Although skepticism was widespread, most Elizabethans firmly believed that witches existed and practiced their evil craft.

It need hardly be pointed out again that Richard functions as God's Scourge, for Hastings also was guilty of heinous crime: he was among those who "stood by" when young Edward of Lancaster was stabbed at Tewkesbury. But Richard remains the most grievous sinner. In this instance he takes vengeance into his own hands. Despite his title of lord protector he has no right to act without due process of law; he makes use of a trumped-up charge.

Sir Richard Ratcliff and Lord William Lovel, whom we meet in this scene, survived to join Catesby as Richard's most confidential ministers during the usurper's short reign. The following lines were affixed to the door of St. Paul's Cathedral on July 18, 1484, at the instigation of William Colyngburne:

> The Cat, the Rat, and Lord our dog
> Ruleth all England under a Hog.

Lovel became the king's chamberlain; Catesby speaker in parliament in

1484; Ratcliff sheriff of Westmorland. The last named was probably closest to Richard, as his role in this play suggests.

In his next-to-last speech (98-103), Hastings moralizes in a completely medieval manner. He pictures himself as one among the many who thoughtlessly sought the "momentary grace of mortal men" rather than "the grace of God." Such reflections are typical of those expressed by the tragic figures in Boccaccio's *De Casibus Virorum Illustrium* and its progeny, including the Elizabethan *Mirror for Magistrates,* which is recognized as one of the sources for Shakespeare's *Richard III.*

ACT III – SCENE 5

Summary

Outside the Tower, Richard and Buckingham come in wearing battered, rusty armor. They are engaged in further deception, namely to pretend that they are in terror of an attack on their lives. Richard instructs Buckingham to speak breathlessly and turn pale, and Buckingham replies that he can counterfeit like an experienced actor. Then the lord mayor enters, brought by Catesby. It is now apparent that the act is put on for his benefit. And it is a good act. The mayor witnesses an excited Richard rushing about as he gives incisive orders for defense against enemies who apparently are about to enter. Buckingham plays his role well enough as he exclaims: "God and innocency defend and guard us!" (20) And then Ratcliff and Lovel — "friends" — enter with Hastings' head.

Richard protests his unsuspecting love for Hastings and talks of having confided in him and of being convinced of his innocence in other things, since he frankly acknowledged his relations with Jane Shore. Richard and Buckingham convince the lord mayor that Hastings had plotted to murder the two of them that day, and that only this extreme peril forced them to execute him before the lord mayor arrived. Gloucester is careful to point out that the "peace of England" as well as their own lives was involved. Even after the mayor wholly agrees that Hastings fully deserved death, Richard protests that Lovel and Ratcliff had carried out his intentions too hastily, for he would have liked the lord mayor to hear the traitor's confession so that he, in turn, could reassure the citizens who might misinterpret Richard's action. After further assurances on both sides, the mayor leaves and Gloucester instructs Buckingham to follow and talk to the citizens at an advantageous moment. He is to imply that Edward IV's children are illegitimate, making the most of the late king's alleged notoriety in matters relating to sex. Further, Buckingham is to suggest that Edward himself was illegitimate. But the latter charge is to be handled skillfully, since Edward's mother survives. Buckingham promises to do his work as well as if he were to gain the crown for himself. Thus having taken the necessary steps to prepare the populace to look on himself as the only true heir to the throne, Richard dispatches Lovel to a priest, Doctor Shaw, and Catesby to Friar Penker; both churchmen are to meet him at Baynard's Castle within the hour. Then he leaves to put Clarence's children out of sight so that no one will have access to them.

Commentary

Here Shakespeare prepares for the scene in which Gloucester is offered the crown. Not without significance is the fact that it reveals a wary Richard who does not take into his confidence Buckingham, the man whom he had called his "other self," his "oracle" and "prophet," his "thought's sovereign."

The stage direction, "Enter Gloucester and Buckingham, in rotten armor, marvellously ill-favored" derives from the First Folio (1623). It follows More's account: "And at their coming, himself [Richard] with the Duke of Buckingham stood harnessed in old ill faring briganders [body armor for foot soldiers], such as no man should when that they would vouchsafe to put on their backs except that some sudden necessity had constrained them." Obviously the two have dressed themselves appropriately for the roles they are about to play for the benefit of the Lord Mayor of London—that is, to make him believe that their concern is for the safety of the state.

At the beginning of this scene we find Gloucester schooling Buckingham in the devices and methods of the Machiavellian villain. And Buckingham proves to be an apt pupil. His first speech (5-11) incorporates an interesting bit of dramatic criticism, a commentary on "ham" acting. This play is sufficiently melodramatic, one which lends itself to the rhetorical school of acting with all its excesses. But Shakespeare tells us thus early in his career that he recognizes such acting for what it is. It should be recalled that he himself was an actor as well as a playwright. The student will find relevant a more famous expression of dramatic criticism written by the mature Shakespeare in *Hamlet,* III.ii.1-40.

The lord mayor was Sir Edmund Shaw (or Shaa), who had been elected in 1482. History reports that he indeed took an active part in influencing the succession of the crown on the death of Edward IV. The grateful Richard later made him a privy councilor. Doctor Shaw, whom Gloucester sends for at the end of the scene, was the lord mayor's brother. He was chosen by Richard to preach a sermon at St. Paul's Cross on June 22, 1483, wherein he impugned the validity of Edward IV's marriage to Elizabeth Woodville and even asserted that Edward and Clarence were bastards. More states that both Shaw and Friar Penker were great preachers, but adds that both were "of more learning than virtue, of more fame than learning." He further states that the brothers Shaw were taken into the confidence of Richard and Buckingham after Hastings' death.

ACT III – SCENE 6

Summary

In this very brief scene a scrivener reads the indictment of Hastings which he has just copied so that it may be given a public reading at St. Paul's Cathedral without delay. It had taken him eleven hours to copy the original draft, which must have taken quite as long to prepare. Yet Hastings was executed only five hours ago. Obviously the whole proceeding is unjust. But the scribe departs, commenting that anyone with sense enough to see what is going on must also have sense enough to keep quiet about it.

Commentary

Although the audience already is fully aware of why Hastings has been rushed to his death, Shakespeare chose to emphasize the complete illegality of Richard's action. He does so here by introducing the professional writer of legal documents with his undramatic but pointed speech. Like the lengthy exchange between Clarence and his murderers (I.iv), the scene underscores the fact that the Shakespeare of *Richard III* was especially interested in the theme of revenge and develops it from more than one point of view (cf. Lily B. Campbell, *Shakespeare's "Histories,"* 1947, pp. 312-13). Further, the scrivener gives expression to what has been called "the smothered feeling of indignation that boils in men's minds under a tyrannical dynasty" (C. C. Clarke, *Shakespeare's Characters,* 1863, p. 470). Recall how Shakespeare had used the three London citizens for a comparable purpose in Act II, scene iii.

ACT III – SCENE 7

Summary

Buckingham, returned from haranguing the mob, meets Richard at Baynard's Castle, as had been arranged. Richard asks at once about the reactions of the London citizens. Buckingham reports that they were silent, and goes on to describe his own recital of Edward's engagements to

Lady Lucy and the sister-in-law of the King of France before his marriage. He contrasted Edward's dissimilarity to their father and Richard's likeness, and went on to dwell upon Richard's 'discipline in war, wisdom in peace;... bounty, virtue, fair humility." When they said nothing, he asked the mayor the cause of their silence. The mayor explained that they were used to be spoken to on public matters only by the recorder, the chief legal authority of the City of London. At Buckingham's insistence, the recorder did report Buckingham's argument, but took care to indicate that he was not speaking for himself. When he had finished, ten of Buckingham's paid followers cried, "God save King Richard!" Taking advantage of this, the duke thanked the multitude for their applause, complimented them on their wisdom, and came away. Buckingham explains that the mayor is coming and advises Richard to pretend to be afraid and to answer only after much urging. Richard is to retreat with two churchmen, while Buckingham makes out a case for his holiness. Above all, Richard is to appear most reluctant when he is requested to accept the crown. As a knock at the door is heard, Gloucester goes up the "leads" (the flat roof top) to prepare himself for his latest and perhaps most challenging role.

The mayor and the citizens enter, followed by Catesby, who tells them that Richard, "divinely bent to meditation," is in the company of "two right reverend Fathers," and begs them to return tomorrow or the next day thereafter. Buckingham then directs Catesby to plead with Richard to come and talk with them. While Catesby is gone, the duke takes the opportunity to point up the contrast of Richard's holy occupation with the late king's self-indulgence. He concludes with apparent fear that Richard will not accept the kingship. "Marry, God forbid His Grace should say us nay!" exclaims the mayor. Catesby comes back with the timely message that Richard is apprehensive as to the reason for the delegation which waits upon him. Again Catesby departs to convey Buckingham's reassurance. Just as the duke finishes a comment on the religiosity of men like Richard, the lord protector himself appears above, standing between two clergyman — "Two props of virtue for a Christian Prince," as Buckingham is quick to point out. The duke implores Richard to pardon them for interrupting him in his holy devotions and to listen to their request. The soul of humility, Richard protests that it is he who is at fault for neglecting his friends. Or, he continues, he may have been guilty unwittingly of greater offense. Buckingham follows this cue: Richard's fault is his failure to rescue the country by becoming king at this time of crisis.

In a nicely contrived refusal, Gloucester protests that he would turn away in reproof, except that they might misinterpret his action as "Tongue-tied ambition." He argues that, even though he were to receive the crown as his due, he does not consider himself to be worthy of such greatness; fortunately the young prince, who merits the crown, will receive it in due course. According to Buckingham this nicety of conscience shows his integrity. But, he points out, the prince cannot be the real heir, since Edward married his mother when she was a widow and Edward himself betrothed successively to Lady Lucy and to Bona, sister of the King of France. Thus, only by courtesy is young Edward called the prince; it is Richard's duty to save the kingship from an impure line. The mayor, Buckingham once more, Catesby — all plead with him, but again Richard refuses. Buckingham lauds him for the compassion and nobility that cause him to refuse, but points out that they will not accept the prince in any case, so that Richard's refusal would mean the downfall of the house of York. "Come, citizens," he concludes. "'Zounds! I'll entreat no more." Gloucester greets this with a pious injunction against swearing. When Catesby and one of the citizens urge him to call them back and accept, he does so sorrowfully.

Richard is at pains to make clear that he is accepting the burden on their entreaty, though to do so goes against his conscience. All have returned to the stage now, and Richard tells them that they must shoulder the blame if he does not fulfill his office well, since they urged him to it. Buckingham salutes him with the title of king and promptly suggests that the coronation take place the very next day. "Even when you please," says Richard, "since you will have it so." The arrangements having been concluded, they depart. And Richard returns to his "holy meditations."

Commentary

It may be argued that this final scene of Act III is quite as contrived as is the scene in which Richard woos and wins Lady Anne (I.ii), but in its way it is no less entertaining and theatrically effective. The element of suspense is first introduced. We learn that Buckingham has followed his directions to the letter, but that there is little evidence of popular support for Richard, who inveighs against the citizens, calling them "tongueless blockheads." Yet this apparent setback is really a challenge which, ably assisted by Buckingham and Catesby, he meets successfully. He succeeds in making the mayor and his group believe that the office seeks the man, not the man the office; and that they must assume responsibility accordingly. The arrival of the mayor, *et al.*, and the dramatic appearance of Richard aloft, standing between two bishops, provide first-rate spectacle.

Much already has been said about Richard's superior intellect and cunning; his entire performance in this scene substantiates all that. But Buckingham's accomplishments must not be ignored. As a matter of fact, they add to those of Gloucester, who picked and schooled him in the art of dissembling. Here Buckingham proves himself capable enough to coach his master on how to present himself to the lord mayor and the citizens. The duke has even picked up Richard's trick of using pious oaths, as when he swears "by the holy Mother of Our Lord" (2) which, in context, is deeply ironical.

Once more much is made of the allegation that Edward IV's heirs are not legitimate. Lady Elizabeth Lucy had been one of the king's mistresses, but there is no record of a betrothal, despite Buckingham's assertion that the Duchess of York had been a witness to such a ceremony (180). But all chroniclers agree that Edward was secretly married to Elizabeth Woodville when the Earl of Warwick had already succeeded in obtaining King Louis of France's consent to the marriage of the Lady Bona. These events are dramatized in *Henry VI, Part Three,* III.iii. In accordance with canon law which prevailed before the Reformation, Edward could not have married Elizabeth Woodville legally. But, of course, Edward remained in England and may not have had news of Warwick's action. More telling is the accusation of "loathed bigamy" (189). Bigamy, defined as either marrying two virgins successively, or once marrying a widow, had been declared unlawful and infamous by canon law in the thirteenth century. The reader will recall, however, that Lady Anne was a widow when Richard wooed her. The essential point is that Buckingham marshals every possible argument in an attempt to prove that Richard is the rightful heir to the throne.

It should be understood that when he salutes Richard as "England's royal king" (240), he is using the term *royal* in a very special sense well understood by Shakespeare's generation. It meant that Richard was not merely royal in rank, having been chosen king, but royal in descent. Essential to Richard's purpose is that he be accepted as a lawful king, not as a usurper.

ACT IV – SCENE 1

Summary

This scene opens with a gathering of those whom Richard has wronged and who will suffer far more acutely in the future. Queen Elizabeth, the old Duchess of York, and Dorset enter from one side. They are on their way to visit the princes in the Tower. At the same moment Richard's wife, Anne, Duchess of Gloucester, comes in leading Clarence's young daughter, Lady Margaret Plantagenet. They are also on their way to the Tower.

As they exchange greetings and make their errands known to one another, Brakenbury enters. Queen Elizabeth immediately asks how the princes are. He replies that they are well, but that the king has ordered that they are to have no visitors. The reference to "the King" appalls Elizabeth, and she demands an explanation. Brakenbury begs her pardon and says that he means the lord protector. The women are now thoroughly alarmed, and each protests that she has special right to see the children. But Brakenbury insists that he cannot violate his oath.

The Earl of Derby (Stanley) enters and greets the Duchess of York as "the looker-on of two fair queens," meaning, of course, Elizabeth and Anne. He has come to escort Anne to Westminster for the coronation. Both women express utter horror at the news. When Dorset tries to comfort his mother, she immediately thinks of his danger and commands him to join Richmond in Brittany. Stanley, stepfather to Richmond (to whom he refers as his son), strongly approves of her counsel. The old duchess curses the womb that brought forth Richard.

Stanley urges Lady Anne to hurry. She replies that she would rather be tortured by the ancient method of encircling her brow with red hot steel than be crowned queen. Elizabeth, so far from being offended at Anne, voices words of commiseration. Anne recalls how she had denounced Richard for making her a widow and had uttered a curse on the woman who married him. Now she realizes that she is the victim of her own curse, for she has not known a moment's rest since her marriage because of Richard's "timorous" dreams. She fears that Richard will do away with her. With grief and foreboding the women part, the old duchess wishing for the grave and Queen Elizabeth remaining behind to look back at the rough outline of the Tower. She prays that it will use her young children well, knowing perhaps too well that her entreaty to the stones is useless.

Commentary

This scene is important chiefly because we get the first hint of a possible turn of events which could lead to Gloucester's downfall. Queen Elizabeth says to Dorset, her son:

> If thou wilt outslip death, go cross the seas,
> And live with Richmond, from the reach of Hell.   (42-43)

This is the first mention of Henry Tudor, Earl of Richmond. Since Shakespeare was dramatizing history, his audiences knew that Richmond would emerge as Richard's nemesis.

It is not without interest that Stanley, who had married the widow of Owen Tudor and is thus Richmond's stepfather, should endorse Elizabeth's advice so emphatically, although it is he who came to escort Anne to Westminster, where Richard is to be crowned King of England. His behavior here is quite consistent with what history tells us about the Stanleys. They had flourished during the entire period of the Wars of the Roses by shifting loyalties when events seemed so to dictate to their advantage and, in the words of Mr. Paul M. Kendall, "by developing an ambiguity of attitude which enabled them to join the winning side, by exploiting the relative facility with which treason in this age might be lived down, provided it were neither too passionate, too overt, nor too damaging" (*op. cit.*, p. 404).

A turning point in the action is indicated also by the report of Richard's "timorous dreams." Here Shakespeare remained quite faithful to his sources. More reported that Gloucester was "sore wearied with care and watch, rather slumbered than slept, troubled with fearful dreams," and that he would sometimes leap out of bed and run about the chamber. Now, since Richard has been established as a Machiavellian villain devoid of conscience, some explanation is called for. It may be argued that conscience does not bother Richard at all, but rather fear for his own life as he wades through blood on his journey to the crown. Or perhaps Stopford Brooke had the right answer: "Shakespeare, with his belief that in the far background of an evil nature the soul lives, but unknown, unbelieved in by its possessor, shows how it awakens at night when the will sleeps, and does its work on the unconscious man. Then, and only then, conscience stirs Richard. Then, and then only, fear besets him" (*On Ten Plays in Shakespeare,* 1905, p. 115). What is most important is that Richard is suffering the unquiet mind. God's justice now is reaching out to him; his doom has begun even before he wears the coveted crown.

Never does Shakespeare let us forget the dominant theme of the play. Anne, who recalls how she had implored God that Richard's wife be made to suffer, again invites divine vengeance on herself when she exclaims

> Anointed let me be with deadly venom,
> And die ere men can say God save the Queen. (62-63)

Certain other points of lesser significance require comment. Note the ritualistic quality of the duchess' farewell addressed successively to Dorset, Anne, and Elizabeth (92-94) — further evidence that the language is highly rhetorical throughout this play. Queen Elizabeth's outburst beginning "Oh, cut my lace in sunder" (34-36) has been cited as an example of sheer rant. But in Tudor England the busks or corsets worn by fashionable women so tightly controlled their figures that one can understand the queen's need for drastic relief in this moment of great emotion.

55

When Anne refers to herself as having been made "so young, so old a widow" (73), she means that she had been made old in sorrow. The Duchess of York, indeed an elderly lady, makes reference to her "eighty odd years" (97). Had her husband lived he would have been just seventy-three; the duchess actually was sixty-eight. Shakespeare purposely exaggerated her age as one means of showing how utterly devoid of virtue Richard was. Reverence for age, particularly for an aged parent, was an essential part of the Elizabethan Order picture. At the family level, as at the political level, Gloucester destroys order.

ACT IV – SCENE 2

Summary

With this scene, the climax of the play has been reached. Richard now wears the coveted crown. He enters the palace in pomp, acknowledges Buckingham, his right-hand man, and tries the duke's loyalty to the utmost by inciting him to arrange for the immediate murder of the little princes. The wary Buckingham does not pick up Richard's indirect suggestion, and the newly crowned king is forced to speak openly: he wishes the "bastards" dead. Now Buckingham's reply is circumspect, and when Richard taunts him, he asks leave to consider. Angry, Richard rails against Buckingham, saying he will speak only to unfeeling and thoughtless boys hereafter. He calls a page over to ask if he knows of anyone who would do murder for money. The page suggests one Tyrrell for whom "gold were as good as orators to tempt." While the page goes to get Tyrrell, the king resolves to confide no more in Buckingham.

Stanley enters with the news that Dorset has fled to Richmond. Without appearing to have heard, Richard orders Catesby to spread the rumor abroad that his wife Anne is ill and likely to die. He will make certain that she sees no one. Meanwhile he must find some commoner to marry and dispose of Clarence's daughter; Clarence's son poses no problem, since he is weak-minded. Richard knows that to murder the princes and then to marry their sister Elizabeth, as he hopes to do, involves great risks:

> Uncertain way of gain! But I am in
> So far in blood that sin will pluck on sin.   (64-65)

Stanley, who had moved to one side, did not hear a word of this heartless speech.

Tyrrel enters and arrangements are made to dispose of the princes, whom Richard describes as foes to his rest and his "sweet sleep's disturbers." Buckingham, having considered the king's suggestion about murdering the children, returns. Richard ignores him and talks to Stanley, warning him to take care, since Richmond is his stepson. The duke interrupts with a request for the rewards he has been promised, especially the earldom of Hereford. The king continues to ignore him. He recalls a prophecy of Henry VI that Richmond would be king, and another made by an Irish bard that Richard himself would not live long after he saw Richmond. As Buckingham again interrupts, Richard asks the time and sarcastically compares the duke to the "Jack" on a clock, a mechanical figure that appears to strike the hour—in just such a way does Buckingham keep begging and interrupting Richard's thoughts. Left alone on the stage, the duke now fully understands his position. Recalling the fate of Hastings, he resolves to flee to his manor at Brecknock, without his rewards but at least with his head.

Commentary

In this climactic scene, wherein Richard enters in state amid the sounding of trumpets, preparation is made for the murder of the little princes, the death of Anne, and the plan for Richard to marry his niece, Elizabeth of York. Even more important is the fact that the newly crowned Richard definitely begins his descent on Fortune's Wheel. Crediting Buckingham for making possible this advancement to the throne, the king asks:

> But shall we wear these honors for a day?
> Or shall they last, and we rejoice in them?   (5-6)

Anne's account of his "timorous dreams" told us that now Richard was a man beset with fears. Like Macbeth he has murdered sleep. And as he explains to Tyrrel, the princes are foes to his rest and his "sweet sleep's disturbers" (74). His words concerning how "sin will pluck on sin," quoted in the summary, anticipate those of Macbeth, the later Shakespearean tragic hero who also willfully embraced evil, driven first by inordinate ambition and then by fear:

> I am in blood
> Stepped in so far that I should wade no more,
> Returning were as tedious as go o'er.
> (*Macbeth*, III.iv. 136-38)

But Buckingham—the "deep-revolving [artful, cunning] witty Buckingham," who had been so pliant heretofore—can not bring himself to be the agent in the murder of the princes. Such utter heartlessness belongs only to Richard, the self-avowed villain who would outdo Machiavel. But surely this is not the sole answer. Buckingham knows quite as well as does Richard that here indeed is "uncertain way to gain."

For Richard the disaffection of Buckingham is the first serious check in his fortunes. Shakespeare develops this part of the scene with consummate skill. When the king says "Edward lives" (10), he expects the duke to reply that Edward will not survive for long. Instead, Buckingham merely says, "True, noble Prince." And Richard's vehement exclamation,

> Oh, bitter consequence,
> That Edward should live true noble Prince!

implies that, in his opinion, the duke is acknowledging the prince's right to the throne.

The news of Dorset's flight to Richmond is additional evidence that Richard has begun his fall. That he should appear to ignore Stanley, who brought him this latest intelligence, and to proceed to instruct Catesby to spread the rumor that Anne "is sick, and like to die," and then to question and instruct the newly arrived Tyrrel as regards the little princes — all this is only new proof of his capacity for prompt action, for dealing with first things first. Earlier commentators suggested that, in view of Richard's words with Catesby, the king himself planned to poison his wife. However, it has been established that Anne was suffering from tuberculosis and that she had been crushed in spirit by the recent death of her son.

Henry VI's prophecy, recalled by Richard in this scene (98-104), is to be found in *Henry VI, Part III*, IV.iv.68-74. The last of the Lancastrian rulers addressed young Richmond as "England's hope" and spoke of him as one "Likely in time to bless a royal throne." It is irrelevant that Richard himself was not present when the words were spoken, although he speaks of himself as "being by." The main thing is that Richmond is becoming an increasingly important figure, the very mention of whose name is ominous to Richard.

ACT IV – SCENE 3

Summary

In soliloquy Tyrrel describes the murder of the children, which has taken place offstage. He is shaken with horror at the very thought of the bloody deed; even the underlings he had hired to do the actual killing melted with compassion. As he retells the story Dighton and Forrest had told him, he describes for the audience the children, sleeping in each other's arms, a prayer book lying on their pillow. For a moment Forrest became conscience-stricken, but recovered himself to join Dighton in smothering the innocent children. Now the latter is conscience-stricken and filled with remorse as he brings his report to the "bloody King."

Richard is pleased to learn that the princes are dead and buried. He instructs Tyrrel to see him after supper and give him all the details and receive the promised reward. As Tyrrel goes out, Richard summarizes his accomplishments. Clarence's son is in prison, his daughter "meanly... matched" in marriage, the princes are dead, Anne has "bid the world goodnight." And now, since Richmond wants to marry young Elizabeth, daughter of Edward IV, Richard must carry out his plan to marry her first. He is about to leave and to present himself to her as a "jolly thriving wooer," when Catesby enters.

Now the mood changes for Richard. Catesby brings the disquieting news that Ely has fled to Richmond and that Buckingham is gathering forces in Wales. The king is more distressed to hear of Ely's withdrawal. The news, however, instead of crushing him, fills him with a zest for battle. Urging speed, he goes off to muster men for the fight.

Commentary

Authentic classical drama never included scenes of violence on the stage but depended upon reports usually made by a messenger. In Elizabethan drama, notably the Seneca of the popular stage, such scenes were presented in full sight of the audience. But Shakespeare was not influenced by classical tradition here. Surely a matter of good taste was involved. The actual scene of the two children being put to death would have been intolerable even for audiences nurtured on scenes of violence. Actually, Tyrrel's recital is far more effective as a means of arousing the emotions of pity and horror. The utter bestiality of the crime is first emphasized by identifying Dighton and Forrest as "two fleshed villains, bloody dogs" — that is, they are like vicious animals which have been allowed to taste human blood. The description of the victims, "those tender babes," more than suffices for Shakespeare's purpose. Now we are fully ready emotionally to witness the bloody king's downfall. Richard's hurried questions — "...am I happy in thy news?"..."But didst thou see them dead?"..."And buried...?" — and his concern to hear all the details of the murders reveal the state of his anxiety.

In the summary of his accomplishments which precedes the bad news he is to receive, we learn that Anne has died and the king is free to marry Elizabeth of York. Holinshed wrote that she died "either by inward thought

and pensiveness, or by infection of poison, which is affirmed most likely."
Richard's public reputation, made clear by the discourse of the two London
citizens (II.iii) is such that, whatever the true facts may be, he is suspect.

Richard, whose intellectuality is never to be underestimated, is percep-
tive enough to realize that, in seeking to marry Elizabeth, Richmond aspires
to wrest the crown from him. Characteristically, he will not delay wooing
her for himself.

John Morton, Bishop of Ely, who was among those present in the
Tower of London to make arrangements for the coronation of Edward V
(III.iv), fled to join Richmond after plotting with Buckingham, according
to Holinshed. News of his flight especially oppresses Richard. But once
more the villain-hero proves himself to be a man of action above all else.
"My counsel is my shield," he exclaims (56); that is, he will waste no time
in deliberation; he will fight.

ACT IV – SCENE 4

Summary

The first part of this scene, a long lament, opens appropriately with old
Queen Margaret saying that she has lurked about and watched the waning
of her adversaries. She is going to withdraw to France, confident that everything will continue as badly as it has begun. Queen Elizabeth enters with
the Duchess of York, weeping for her children. Margaret declares that the
loss is a deserved one, since Edward IV, the children's father, had been a
principal in the murder of Margaret's son Edward. When Elizabeth asks
her when she could sleep when the little princes had been put to death,
Margaret replies bitterly: "When holy Harry died, and my sweet son." The
duchess, overcome with her own woes, sits down on the ground that has
been "made drunk with innocents' blood." Elizabeth wishes that the earth
would open up and offer her a grave as easily as it offers her a seat.

Queen Margaret joins them, insisting that her sorrows have precedence,
since they are the oldest. She begins a long recital of their joint woes, identifying Richard III as the author. The Duchess of York interrupts to accuse
Margaret of being responsible for the deaths of her husband (Richard, Duke
of York) and Rutland, one of her sons. Margaret continues, insisting that
the deaths of Edward IV, the young princes, and Clarence were debts paid
for crimes committed against the house of Lancaster. So died the "be-
holders of this tragic play," Hastings, Rivers, Vaughan, and Grey – yet
Richard, "Hell's black intelligencer," still lives. She utters a prayer that
she may yet survive to say "The dog is dead."

Elizabeth recalls Margaret's prophecy that the time would come when she would ask for Margaret's help in cursing Richard, "That bottled spider, that foul-backed toad!" Margaret reminds her of what she had said at greater length about Elizabeth. She compares Elizabeth to a flag borne by a standard-bearer which attracts all shots:

> Where is thy husband now? Where be thy brothers?
> Where are thy children? Wherein dost thou joy?
> Who sues to thee, and cries "God save the Queen"?
>
> (92-94)

Just as Elizabeth once usurped her place as queen, so now she usurps a just share of Margaret's sorrow. When she is about to leave after this tirade, Elizabeth asks her to stay and teach her how to curse. Margaret gives her a grim recipe, and, on further urging, points out that woe will teach Elizabeth what she wants to know. Finally she leaves. The duchess asks why calamity should be so full of words. Elizabeth describes them as "Windy attorneys to their clients woes" which "Help not at all, yet do they ease the heart." The duchess urges Elizabeth to accompany her and smother Richard in the breath of bitter words, since he had smothered Elizabeth's children. At this point the king himself enters, marching, with drums and trumpets.

Richard asks who intercepts his march, whereupon the duchess and Elizabeth attack him for his wrongs. He threatens to drown his mother's words in a flourish of trumpets unless she speaks fair of him. When he shows his impatience, she states that she can think of no single hour, from his birth onward, when he has not been a source of trouble to her. She warns him that, though this is their last meeting, she leaves him with a "heavy curse": may his adversaries crush him: "Bloody thou art, bloody will be thine end." Elizabeth voices her amen to all that the duchess has said, but Richard nevertheless detains her.

When Elizabeth states that she has no more sons for Richard to murder and that her daughters will be "praying nuns, not weeping queens," the king begins his suit for the hand of her daughter Elizabeth, whom he praises as "Virtuous and fair, royal and gracious." Understandably, the queen-mother wonders what new torture Richard has in store for her, and she is provoked into a violent harangue against him. He protests that he means to do her good—he will marry her daughter if she will only forget past grievances and give her consent. Elizabeth is horrified. When he asks how to go about winning the young lady, she bitterly suggests that he has done everything calculated to win a girl's heart—murdered her brothers, her aunt (Anne), her uncles (Clarence and Rivers). Making use of all of his persuasive powers, the king claims that what is done cannot be undone; that he will make up for the loss of the princes, her children, by making her daughter the mother of kings and herself the happy grandmother. Elizabeth obviously is moved by the proposal and agrees to let him know her daughter's mind shortly. This jolly, thriving wooer asks her to bear to the girl his "true love's kiss." Once she has left, however, he refers to Elizabeth with amusement: "Relenting fool, and shallow, changing woman!"

Ratcliff and Catesby come with the news that Richmond, with a powerful navy, is off the coast of Wales waiting for Buckingham's support. Richard orders Catesby to go immediately to the Duke of Norfolk, and Ratcliff to leave for Salisbury. Not until he has upbraided Catesby for delaying does he become aware of the fact that he had neglected to give instructions. Norfolk is to be told to raise the greatest possible "strength and power" and to meet Richard at Salisbury.

Lord Stanley (Derby) enters with the news that Richmond, aroused by Dorset, Buckingham, and Ely, "makes for England, there to claim the crown." Richard asks why should this be, since the royal throne is occupied and no other heir of York survives. He accuses Stanley of planning to rebel against him and fly to his enemies. Stanley protests that he is loyal to Richard and promises to bring his forces down from the north. But the king still does not trust him; he insists that Stanley leave his son George as assurance of his loyalty.

As Stanley leaves, messengers enter successively with news of the revolt of Courtney and the Bishop of Exeter in Devonshire, and of the Guilfords in Kent — that is, risings in the southeast and southwest parts of the kingdom. Furious, Richard strikes the third messenger before he has a chance to speak, and then learns that this time the news is good: Buckingham's forces have been dispersed by flood. Still another messenger reports that Sir Thomas Lovel and Dorset head a force in Yorkshire to the north. But this bad news for Richard is offset by the report that Richmond, his fleet broken up by a tempest and mistrusting those on shore who said they came from Buckingham, has hoisted sail and made for Brittany.

Catesby comes in to say that Buckingham has been captured, but that Richmond had landed with a "mighty power" at Milford. "Away for Salisbury!" exclaims Richard. There is no time to reason: "A royal battle might be won and lost." His final order is that Buckingham be brought to Salisbury.

Commentary

In this scene Queen Margaret makes her last appearance and once more, in a completely ritualistic manner, "tells o'er [the Yorkist] woes again" by viewing her own. Her grim forebodings are now being fully realized, and she stresses that mathematical kind of justice which is involved — an eye for an eye, a tooth for a tooth. Probably most would agree with the Duchess of York. Queen Margaret *does* represent "Blind sight, dead life" (26); but she is also the "Brief abstract and record of tedious days" (28), the grim commentator upon bloody deeds who never tires of pointing out the inevitability of God's punishment for grievous sins. As we follow her long discourse, which is briefly interrupted twice, we might well ask as does the Duchess of York: "Why should calamity be full of words?" (126) But Shakespeare forestalls criticism of Margaret's extreme volubility by providing Queen Elizabeth's explanation. In *Henry VI, Part Three,* this same Margaret, having just witnessed the slaughter of her princely son, had said:

> No, no, my heart will burst an if I speak;
> And I will speak that so my heart will burst.
> (V.v.58-59)

So in *Titus Andronicus,* the titular hero, who had sought to ransom his captive sons by cutting off his hand as directed and sending it to the emperor, voiced similar thoughts:

> Then give me leave, for losses will have leave
> To ease their stomachs with their bitter tongues.
> (III.i.233-34)

And in *Macbeth,* written late in Shakespeare's career, Malcolm counsels the distraught Macduff, who has just learned that his wife and children have been killed:

> Give sorrow words. The grief that does not speak
> Whispers the o'er-fraught heart and bids it break.
> (IV.iii.208-09)

The main thing, however, is that in her recital Margaret brings focus upon Richard as the arch-criminal:

> I had an Edward — till a Richard killed him.
> I had a Harry — till a Richard killed him.
> Thou hadst an Edward — till a Richard killed him.
> Thou hadst a Richard — till a Richard killed him.
> (40-43)

Granted that later she indicts Edward IV and Clarence, along with Hastings, Rivers, Vaughan, and Grey. But the emphasis remains on the villain-hero who "yet lives" (71), the recipient of Margaret's most vehement curses. Once she leaves the stage, the Duchess of York and Queen Elizabeth read the catalogue of Richard's crimes in ritualistic manner, now addressing the king himself. The force of the Duchess' words

> Bloody thou art, bloody will be thy end.
> Shame serves thy life and doth thy death attend.
>
> (194-95)

strikes home when one recalls her blessing of her son early in the play. Whether present or absent, then, Richard remains the center of interest.

As the king urges the queen-mother to let him marry her daughter, he argues that he will advance her "to the dignity and height of honor, the high imperial type of this earth's glory" (243-44). Here indeed is the key to Richard's own ambition which drove him to extreme cruelty and bloodshed. He was beset with the same "thirst and sweetness of a Crown" which motivated Marlowe's Tamberlaine and which made Macbeth willing "to jump the life to come."

There are similarities between this wooing scene and the earlier one. For example, at one point the king says: "Say I did all this for love of her," when Elizabeth denounces him for the murders of Clarence and Lord Rivers (281-88). Moreover, the same kind of one-line speeches (*stichomythia*) serves to link the two wooing scenes. Finally, Richard's last words (431) are somewhat reminiscent of those he spoke just after Anne had left him. How do the scenes differ? Chiefly in that sardonic humor finds no place in this later scene: tragic gloom now pervades the action.

This has been called an "outrageous courtship." And so it is. In the chronicle histories, both Hall and Holinshed are appalled at the queen's inconstancy. They record that the queen-mother had already promised the princess to Richmond and later was persuaded by Richard to grant his suit. It may be added that in these prose histories Elizabeth even sends orders for Dorset to desert Richmond and return to England. But not until the next scene does Shakespeare let us know that the queen has "heartily consented to the match with Richmond." Mr. J. Dover Wilson is quite right in saying that "it is rather strange that Shakespeare should leave his audience in doubt for over a hundred and twenty lines whether or no the ancestress of his own Queen Elizabeth had sold her daughter to a man whose hands were red with blood of her sons…"(*Richard III*, Cambridge, 1954, p. xliv).

Judged solely by the action in this scene, Queen Elizabeth may indeed be a "shallow, changing woman" who is moved by selfish ambition. Or one may argue that she saw in such a match the only chance to bring an end to the bloody strife. Did not Richard argue:

> Without her, follows to this land and me,
> To thee, herself, and many a Christian soul,
> Death, desolation, ruin and decay.
>
> (407-09)

If the villain refers to "this land" first, he makes reference to himself before he mentions others who will suffer. But perhaps Elizabeth is no less concerned about her own fate than is the egotistical Richard.

Again one must anticipate Elizabeth's action in scene V. Mr. J. Dover Wilson himself joins the many other critics in concluding that Shakespeare intended us to believe that Richard is tricked in this, his second courtship. That this interpretation would seem to be the correct one is consistent with what we learn in Richard's talk with Catesby, Ratcliff, Stanley, and the messengers. Clearly he is losing his grip on himself. Note how he fails to instruct Catesby and how he changes his mind about Ratcliff's mission. Most of the news is bad now. As Richard hears the tidings, he cries: "Out on you, owls..." (509). The owl, of course, is a symbol and portent of death.

There is one piece of good news for Richard. Buckingham's army has been dispersed and scattered by sudden floods. A bit later we learn that the duke himself has been captured. How does this fit into the scheme of things? Buckingham is a perjurer and an accessory to murder; it would not do to have him survive and fight on the side of righteousness. Again we recall Margaret's dire prophecy when Buckingham ignored her counsel and allied himself with one upon whom "Sin, death, and Hell have set their marks" (I.iii.297-301). No Tudor loyalist would have failed to see divine intervention evident in the sudden floods which were the immediate cause of Buckingham's downfall.

The latter part of this scene provides a good illustration of how Shakespeare telescoped historical events for his purpose. Richard did lead a force toward Salisbury to meet Buckingham in October, 1483. Cut off from his Welsh levies, Buckingham was captured and put to death on October 31. Shortly thereafter, Richmond embarked from Brittany with an invading army; but his ships were dispersed by a storm. He did appear in one vessel off Poole. Richard, endeavoring to lure him ashore, sent false information to the effect that the troops ashore were led by Buckingham.

But Richmond did not fall into the trap; instead he returned to France. Not until two years later did he invade England. To help him repel this invasion, Richard sent for the Duke of Norfolk.

ACT IV – SCENE 5

Summary

Derby (Lord Stanley) sends Sir Christopher Urswick to his stepson Richmond with the message that his son George is held captive. For fear of causing his son's death, Derby cannot send aid to Richmond immediately. He learns that Richmond now is in Wales. Supporting the claimant to the throne are many "of noble fame and worth." They are headed for London. Derby finally instructs Sir Christopher to tell Richmond that the Queen-Mother Elizabeth heartily has given her consent to the marriage of Richmond and her daughter.

Commentary

The powerful forces mustered to oppose Richard are identified. Those who will join Richmond are led by such nobles as Sir Walter Herbert, son of the Earl of Pembroke, who had been a staunch Yorkist; Sir Gilbert Talbot, uncle to the Earl of Shrewsbury; and Sir William Stanley, Derby's brother. Derby's real feelings toward Richard are finally made clear, although he dares not openly oppose the king. Thus, by the end of this act, Richard is supported only by Ratcliff, Catesby, and Lovel. That Richard's last stratagem has failed is also revealed: Elizabeth of York will marry Richmond.

Derby's reference to Richard as "this most bloody boar" emphasizes the king's heartless cruelty which has led him to the brink of ruin. The student will recall that, in Act I, scene iii, Anne had denounced him as a "hedgehog," the first insulting reference to Richard's crest of the wild boar. In Act I, scene iv, the villain-hero had referred to Clarence as being "franked up to fattening for his pains." A frank is a sty for fattening hogs. But it is Richard himself, of course, who is bestial. Here, in the lines assigned to Derby, Shakespeare sustains the metaphor.

ACT V – SCENE 1

Summary

As Buckingham is led to his execution at Salisbury, he is told that Richard will not grant him an audience. He thinks of Henry VI, Henry's son Edward, Hastings, Rivers, Grey, Vaughan, and others who had died "By underhand corrupted foul justice." If from the other world they view his plight, he continues, let them mock his fate. It is All Souls' Day, and he recalls that on another such sacred day he had given Edward IV his pledge to remain at peace with the dying king's children and the queen's allies, inviting God's punishment if he broke that pledge. He then recalls Margaret's curse when he had scoffed at her warning. "Wrong hath but wrong, and blame the due of blame," he concludes. He is saying that this unjust death is only retribution for the unjust deaths he has been responsible for.

Commentary

According to Holinshed (who follows Hall closely here), Buckingham made a full confession in the hope that Richard would agree to see him. He "sore desired" the meeting whether "to sue for pardon...or whether he being brought to his presence would have sticked him with a dagger." The execution actually took place in Shrewsbury.

This scene again makes apparent that throughout the play Shakespeare never lets one lose sight of the major theme: the execution of God's judgment on those guilty of perjury and murder. To Buckingham's credit, let it be said, he acknowledges his own guilt, and his words add up to a justification of God's ways to man.

ACT V – SCENE 2

Summary

The scene shifts to Richmond's camp near Tamworth. Richmond, entering with drums and trumpets, addresses his "Fellows in arms" and "most loving friends," inciting them against Richard, "that wretched, bloody, and usurping boar," who has placed upon them the "yoke of tyranny" and has despoiled their "summer fields and fruitful vines." He acknowledges the receipt of good news from Lord Stanley and reports that Richard is at Leicester, only one day away. In God's name, he urges them on. Oxford and Herbert predict that all Richard's friends will desert him, since they are only friends through fear. "All for our vantage," exclaims Richmond, and again invoking God's name he commands them to march onward.

Commentary

This is a scene that could easily be cut out. Shakespeare included it as essential to the theme he develops throughout the play and to point up Richmond's virtures. From a political point of view, never to be ignored in the chronicle history plays, Shakespeare now teaches the orthodox lesson: Richmond is the rightful heir to the throne, moving against a usurper and murderer. He fights in God's name to save England from the ravages of one who, for a time, had been permitted to function as the Scourge of God.

ACT V – SCENE 3

Summary

On Bosworth Field, Richard, fully armed, enters with Norfolk, the Earl of Surrey, and others. He orders that their tents be pitched. When Richard chides Surrey for looking sad, the earl assures him that his heart is light. Then the king rallies Norfolk, who agrees that they must take blows as well as receive them. Richard states that he will rest here for the night; where he will rest tomorrow, he knows not. Philosophically he adds: "Well, all's one for that." He has reason to be confident, for he learns that his forces outnumber Richmond's three to one. With characteristic vigor, he gives commands preparatory to the battle and calls for men of competent leadership.

On the other side of the field Richmond enters, accompanied by several distinguished nobles. While some soldiers are pitching his tent, Richmond takes note of the sunset, which gives promise of a fair day tomorrow. Calling for ink and paper, he plans the deposition of his forces for the battle. Before parting from the rest, he sends Captain Blount off with an important message to Stanley, whose forces lie about half a mile south of the king's. As they withdraw into the tent to finish the battle plans, Richard, with Norfolk, Ratcliff, Catesby, and others, claim our attention.

It is now nine o'clock, and time for the evening's repast; but Richard decides not to sup. His thoughts are solely on the fight with Richmond. He calls for ink and paper; he asks if his armor is in readiness; he orders Norfolk to check the sentinels. Next, the king instructs Catesby to send a herald's officer to Stanley, ordering that lord to bring his regiment before morning unless he wants his son's head to be forfeit. He asks about the "melancholy Lord Northumberland" and is somewhat cheered to hear that the earl and Surrey have gone among the soldiers encouraging them. But Richard concedes that his own spirits lack alacrity and his mind its wonted cheerfulness. Therefore, he calls for a bowl of wine. Having instructed Ratcliff to come about the middle of the night to arm him, the king asks to be left alone.

Now attention is attracted to Richmond, who is in his tent with various lords and attendants. Derby (Lord Stanley) enters, and the two exchange greetings. Derby brings blessings from Richmond's mother, who prays constantly for her son's welfare. He counsels Richmond to put his fortunes to the test in tomorrow's battle, but explains that in view of his son's plight, he cannot openly join the claimant's forces. Regretting that the encroaching battle prevents them from more time together, Stanley leaves. Richmond prepares himself for sleep, aware that he must be rested before he fights the good fight. Alone, he solemnly prays for God's good will, and to Him he commends his "watchful soul."

As both Richard and Richmond sleep, they are visited by a procession of ghosts of those the king had killed. They come in order of their deaths —Prince Edward, Henry VI, Clarence, Rivers, Grey, Vaughan, the little princes, Hastings, Lady Anne, and Buckingham. Each ghost appears to Richard as an image of retribution, indicting him for his crime and telling him to "despair and die." In the words of Anne, each fills his sleep with perturbations. In contrast, each ghost offers praise and words of comfort to the sleeping Richmond: let him "live and flourish," for good angels guard him and fight on his side. The ghost of Hastings especially urges him to "Arm, fight, and conquer, for fair England's sake!" And the two princes urge him to "Live, and beget a happy race of kings!"

As the ghosts vanish, Richard starts out of his sleep. He has been dreaming of "bloody deeds and death." He cries out for a horse and for someone to bind his wounds. Realizing that he has been dreaming and that he is a victim of "coward conscience," he goes through a self-examination that ends in bitter condemnation of isolated and unpitied guilt. Ratcliff enters to rouse him for battle. Still unnerved, he tells Ratcliff his dream. Ratcliff tries to rally him, and Richard turns his mind to the question of his followers' loyalty. He leaves with Ratcliff to eavesdrop at their tent and see if any mean to shrink from him.

Attention is now directed to Richmond's tent, where nobles enter to greet their leader. He has rested well, having enjoyed the "sweetest sleep and fairest-boding dreams." He tells the lords how the souls of Richard's victims had come to his tent and "cried in victory." Told that it is now four o'clock in the morning, Richmond replies that it is "time to arm and give direction." There follows his formal address to his soldiers.

"God and our good cause fight on our side, he assures the troops, and adds that the "prayers of holy saints and wronged souls" stand before their faces. Even Richard's followers, he continues, want him to be defeated.

Denouncing the king as "A bloody tyrant and homicide," Richmond urges his men to fight against God's enemies and their country's foes. Then may they expect to thrive in a prospering land, their wives and children free from danger. Richmond declares that he himself will fight unto death if necessary. If he wins, all will share in the gain. He calls for drums and trumpets to sound "boldly and cheerfully." And with the stirring cry, "God and Saint George! Richmond and victory!" he leads the way offstage.

It is Richard's turn now to receive full attention. He asks what Northumberland has said of Richmond and is pleased to hear Ratcliff tell him that the earl thinks very little of Richmond's capacity as a soldier and that Surrey was no less pleased with Northumberland's opinion. Richard then asks the time of day. He takes notice of the weather and remarks that the sun should have risen an hour ago. At first Richard is dashed by the thought that the skies are lowering down on him, but he realizes that the sun is not shining on Richmond either. Aroused from these thoughts by Norfolk, Richard tells that noble his plan of battle. A vanguard of horse and foot is to be spread out in front, with archers in the midst. Norfolk and Surrey are to command the foot and horse. Richard will follow in the main battle, his power on each side well-winged with foot and horse. Norfolk approves all this, but passes Richard a taunting note he has found on his tent that morning. Richard dismisses it from his mind and sends his captains to their commands. He is determined not to let "babbling dreams" disturb his soul nor his conscience to bother him. Strong arms will be his conscience and swords his law:

> March on, join bravely, let us to't pell-mell —
> If not to Heaven, then hand in hand to Hell.   (312-13)

In his oration, to the troops, Richard denounces the enemy as a pack of foreign vagabonds and robbers who threaten to devastate the land and attack wives and daughters. He makes much of their being French, reminding his soldiers that their fathers had beaten the French on French soil. He concludes with a stirring call to arms. At this moment, a messenger comes, saying that Stanley refuses to bring his forces in. Richard wants to have young George's head cut off at once, but is persuaded to wait until after the battle, since the enemy are already past the marsh. Crying "A thousand hearts are great within my bosom" and invoking the name of Saint George, the king charges into action.

Commentary

Here Shakespeare especially remained quite faithful to Hall and Holinshed in his account of Richard and Richmond just before the Battle of

Bosworth Field. Now, so near to the end of the play, the conflict has become completely centralized. Early there is evidence that Richard's downfall may be imminent. Surrey looks sad, and his insistence that he is really light of heart is not convincing. A bit later the king inquires about the "melancholy Northumberland." He has reason to be doubtful about that noble. Holinshed reported that Richard suspected him, and later wrote that, when it came to fighting, Northumberland stood aside "with a great company and intermitted not in the battle." And Lord Stanley still poses a problem for the king. Nevertheless, Richard's soldierly courage is apparent, as when he says,

> Here will I lie tonight.
> But where tomorrow? Well, all's one for that.   (7-8)

More to the point is Norfolk's report that Richmond's forces are far outnumbered by Richard's.

Richmond, having risen from "sweetest sleep," is in his tent carefully drawing up his plan of battle. He makes reference to his "small strength," but says nothing that suggests doubt or fear. In fact, his opening lines reflect confidence and peace of mind:

> The weary sun hath made a golden set,
> And by the bright track of his fiery car
> Gives signal of a goodly day tomorrow.   (19-21)

Richmond's prayer, voiced in formal, impressive language, is anything but humble in tone. To understand its full import, one must take the historical point of view. The most obvious point to make is that Shakespeare was writing about Elizabeth I's grandfather, the first of the Tudors, whose claim to the throne had never been wholly secure. Richmond is moving against the man who wears the crown. Throughout the sixteenth century and beyond, the doctrine of absolute obedience to the ruler was inculcated. Even if, like Richard of this play, he was a usurper and murderer, no subject legitimately could rebel against him. In *Richard II*, written two years later, the wise old John of Gaunt, uncle to the king and a voice of orthodoxy, replies to the Duchess of Gloucester, who has implored him to avenge the murder of her husband, Gaunt's brother, a crime attributed to Richard II:

> God's is the quarrel, for God's substitute,
> His deputy anointed in His sight,
> Hath caused his death. The which if wrongfully,
> Let Heaven avenge, for I may never lift
> An angry arm agains His minister (I.ii.37-41)

Granted that Richard II was not an arch-criminal as is Richard III. But, according to the accepted doctrine, it was through God's sufferance that Richard III wore the crown; he functioned, for a time, as has been stated earlier, as the Scourge of God. Now his time to be scourged approaches. Richmond presents himself as God's captain and prays that he and his followers may be "Thy ministers of chastisement." In other words, he now becomes the instrument of God's justice. Thus heralded, the ghosts appear, bringing blessings to Richmond ("Live and flourish!") and curses on Richard ("Despair and die!").

Admittedly the verse in this "ghost" part of the scene is mediocre; in such pageant-like scenes Shakespeare never achieved his best poetry. His aim was to make the most telling use of the supernatural as a way of keeping his major theme to the fore. Since the ghosts appear in the order of their deaths, Shakespeare recapitulates, crime by crime, the whole catalogue. Richard's sleep indeed is filled "with perturbations," to use Anne's phrase. And as the last ghost vanishes, the king wakes in terror and calls for another horse. He has dreamed prophetically that "white Surrey" has been killed under him. His waking thoughts relate directly to the last words spoken by the ghost of Buckingham.

Things have come full circle now. Richard is a deeply troubled soul in contrast to Richmond, God's captain. When he first appeared in the play, the villain-hero revealed his over-powering egotism; he gloated that he was "subtle, false, and treacherous"; he had expressed his determination "to prove a villain." He spoke these words with an insolence that showed him to be utterly devoid of conscience. Now his words appear as overwhelming reproof as he makes his first—and last—homage to moral law. Especially the horror of his isolation from humanity oppresses him: "There is no creature loves me, And if I die no soul shall pity me" (200-201).

"Cowardice conscience" afflicts him. Only when he slept and will was dormant could conscience stir. In that sense it was cowardly. But so vivid had been his dream that he cannot immediately escape conscience even when he wakes: "O Ratcliff, I fear, I fear —," he exclaims. The fact that he feels impelled to eavesdrop on his troops illustrates his faltering confidence.

Richmond's oration to his soldiers requires only brief comment. If there has been any doubt up to this point, now that doubt is resolved: Richmond emerges unmistakably as the divinely appointed champion of justice opposing one who "hath ever been God's enemy." The action now assumes the character of a holy crusade, not against an anointed ruler, but against a bloody tyrant who has enslaved trueborn Englishmen.

When Richard re-enters, he has completely recovered himself. For one thing, it would not do to have the tragic hero collapse before the battle and prove himself to be a straw man. Like Macbeth, that other great criminal, he is the soul of courage, a worthy adversary. Does the sun "disdain to shine" on his army? It does not shine for Richmond either. Richard is his Machiavellian self again: "Conscience is but a word that cowards use," he now exclaims (309).

In the chronicle histories of Hall and Holinshed, Richard was made to confess the murders of the little princes and to express sorrow for the deed when he addressed his army. Not so in Shakespeare's play. In the king's oration there is no place for regrets, despondencies, or sense of violated honor. We have here what has rightly been called "a masterpiece of bold mockery of the foe" (Brooke, *op. cit.*, p. 122). Northumberland had reported that Richmond was "never trained in arms" (272); now Richard refers to his adversary as a "milksop, one that never in his life/ Felt so much cold as over shoes in snow" (325-26). The epithet derives from Holinshed, and Shakespeare makes the most of it. Similarly, Richmond's followers are described in the most contemptuous terms — "overweening rags of France," "famished beggars," "poor rats," "bastard Bretons." No leader could have done more to instill confidence in his troops, to convince them that "Victory sits on our helms." If Richmond is to defeat Richard, God indeed must be on his side.

ACT V — SCENE 4

Summary

The battle is in progress. Catesby is crying to Norfolk to rescue the king, whose horse is slain and who continues to fight on foot. Richard enters, crying out for a horse. Catesby urges him to retire. He refuses, for he is determined to risk all. He leaves this part of the field, still crying for a horse and seeking Richmond.

Commentary

Of chief importance in this scene is evidence of King Richard's unsurpassed courage and martial skill. He is depicted as one "enacting more wonders than a man." From one point of view, this goes far to enhance his stature as the tragic hero; from another point of view, it redounds to Richmond's credit, for the claimant is opposed by one who seems to be superhuman in courage and determination.

Richard's cry ("A horse! A horse! My kingdom for a horse!"), so stirring in context, is the best-known line in the play. It was much admired, quoted, and imitated by his contemporaries. The line does not appear in either Hall or Holinshed. One close to it ("A horse, a horse, a fresh horse") is found in *The True Tragedy of Richard the Third,* a quite inferior version of the villain-hero's rise and downfall which, according to critical consensus, predates Shakespeare's historical tragedy. As Mr. J. Dover Wilson notes, "A stage-entry on horseback being impractical, such a cry was an effective one for a general entering on foot in a battle scene" (*op. cit.,* p. 256).

As regards the "six Richards in the field," Shakespeare employed the same device in *Henry IV, Part One,* wherein several of Henry's knights were dressed like him in the Battle of Shrewsbury. Obviously it was a precaution, since the leader's death often meant defeat.

ACT V – SCENE 5

Summary

As prepared for in the previous scene, Richard and Richmond fight, and Richard is slain. Richmond retreats and returns, receiving the congratulation of his friends for the victory, which is now assured. Derby (Lord Stanley) is carrying the crown, which he has taken from Richard. He places it on the head of Richmond. To the new king's question about young George Stanley (Richmond's half-brother), Derby replies that the youth is safe in Leicester. Richmond asks the names of nobles on both sides who have been slain and orders that they be buried "as becomes their births." In accordance with his wishes, all soldiers who have fled are to be pardoned if they return in submission to him. After taking the sacrament, he will marry Elizabeth of York, Edward IV's daughter, thus uniting the Yorkist and the Lancastrians. The harsh wars which have caused so much grief and injury, even among members of the same family, are now over. God willing, England will enter a reign of peace and prosperity. His concluding words are a prayer that traitors may perish and peace reign, now that civil wounds are healed.

Commentary

Appropriately in the final scene there is a clearing of the moral atmosphere. The "bloody dog" is dead; order is restored. In hand-to-hand combat Richmond slays the adversary who had performed apparently superhuman deeds on the battlefield. Everywhere the new king's moral superiority is emphasized: his concern for George Stanley, his chivalry in ordering that all nobles slain, enemies included, be given proper burial; his proclamation of an amnesty; his profound religiosity. Shakespeare lived and wrote in an England beset with repeated threats to peace: the Northern Rebellion (1569); the Ridolphi Plot (1572); the Babington Plot (1586); attempted foreign invasion and fear of a rising against a queen who had been declared excommunicate and deposed by the Papal Bull of 1570. In official sermon and numerous polemical tracts and ballads the horrors of civil war and the heinous crime of treason were dominant themes. In the latter part of this scene, Shakespeare finds occasion to offer the same doctrine. To Elizabethans especially, Richmond's fervent prayer was most apposite and inspiring.

NOTES ON CHARACTERS

RICHARD, DUKE OF GLOUCESTER, AFTERWARD RICHARD III

Richard is Shakespeare's first villain-hero. Self-acclaimed as one who will "outdo Machiavel," he possesses all of the traits of that Elizabethan stage villain. Primarily he is motivated by boundless ambition to gain and hold the crown, and by his pronounced egotism. Utterly heartless, he does not hesitate to move against his own brothers, arranging for the murder of Clarence, misleading and later slandering Edward IV, and putting to death his own nephews. It is implied in the text that he also poisoned his wife Anne so that the way would be clear for his political marriage to his niece, Elizabeth of York. A master of dissembling and a man obviously not without charm, despite his physical deformity, he deludes Edward IV, for a time convinces Queen Elizabeth and her family that he has no further quarrel with them, and manages to gain the support of the Lord Mayor of London, among others. Add to all this the energy with which he initiates and carries out every action necessary to his gaining the crown and, for a time, retaining it, and one can understand why he dominates the play to an extent to which no other Shakespearean tragic hero does. His soliloquies and asides reveal a Richard who is honest at least with himself. Courage and soldierly prowess also belong to him. Finally, he possesses an unexcelled sense of irony and a sardonic wit which go far to explain his special attraction to audiences and readers.

HENRY, EARL OF RICHMOND, AFTERWARD HENRY VII

Richmond is not heard of until Act IV, scene, i, when Queen Elizabeth urges her son Dorset to save himself by joining Richmond in Brittany. It is true that, in Act I, scene ii, we find a reference to his mother, the Countess Richmond, who is married to Lord Stanley, Earl of Derby; and we learn that the countess has not been friendly to Edward IV's queen. But by the end of Act IV, we learn that "Richmond is on the seas," and he then definitely emerges as Richard III's nemesis. Inevitably, Richmond provides the strongest contrast to Richard. If the latter is "hell's black intelligencer" and "that foul defacer of God's handiwork," Richmond is "God's Captain," the agent of divine justice to be imposed upon Richard. It will not do to criticize him adversely as one who is intolerably stuffy in his proclaimed religiosity and conviction of righteousness. In the words of Mr. J. Dover Wilson, Shakespeare "could hardly have done other than represent Henry of Richmond as a kind of St. George and the king he slays as much like a dragon as a human may be" (*op. cit.*, p. xix).

EDWARD IV

Edward IV appears only briefly in this play. The eldest son of the Duke of York is depicted as one who already is paying for his sins and those of the house of York in general. His reign has been characterized by strife including the Woodville faction and those who bitterly oppose the queen and her family. Edward dies believing that amity has been restored and that the succession of the crown to his son has been assured. He is, then, prominent among those who are deluded by Richard, as the death of Clarence illustrates. The fact that his personal life had been a notorious one, particularly as relates to Jane Shore, worked to Richard's advantage after Edward's death.

GEORGE, DUKE OF CLARENCE

The third son of the Duke of York is Richard's first victim. He is the unhappy, "false, fleeting, perjured Clarence," who learns only just before his violent death that it is his own brother Richard who has plotted against him. His account of his terrifying dream (I.iv) is one of the most memorable parts of the drama. Clarence invites sympathy, not only because we know that he is opposed by an evil monster, but because he acknowledges his guilt, expresses greatest concern for his wife and children, and dies courageously.

HENRY, DUKE OF BUCKINGHAM

Buckingham is ambitious to become the Earl of Hereford and to gain the "movables" of the earldom, brashly ignores Queen Margaret's warning and aligns himself with Richard of Gloucester. He becomes convinced that he is indeed Richard's "second self," his "counsel's consistory," his "oracle" and "prophet." He is at his zenith when he sets the stage and gives the directions for the reception of the lord mayor and the urging of Richard to accept the crown. He sees himself as a second Warwick, a king-maker, and is confident of prompt reward. Not until Richard sounds him out regarding the plan to murder the little princes does Buckingham waver in his unquestioning obedience to the new king. Although he escapes to Wales and raises forces to oppose his former master, he is not allowed to survive, so deep in sin has he fallen.

QUEEN MARGARET OF ANJOU

The widow of Henry VI, one-time vigorous prosecutor of the Lancastrian cause, has survived into old age as a kind of Fury voicing curses and horrible prophecies. In her speeches, so highly rhetorical and formalistic, the major theme of the play receives repeated emphasis. She lives to see, and practically to gloat over, the fulfillment of one curse, one prophecy, after another. It is she who makes understandable why—in accordance with that mathematical scheme of justice which she constantly dwells upon —Queen Elizabeth, the Duchess of York, and even the little princes should suffer.

WILLIAM, LORD HASTINGS

The chamberlain to Edward IV and loyal adherent of the Yorkist cause is also among those deluded by Richard. Because he was a victim of the machinations of the Woodvilles, he understandably first sided with Gloucester, whose protestations of innocence he accepted readily. Hastings long remains supremely confident, blithely ignoring portents of catastrophe. No one could have been more surprised than he when Richard ordered that he be seized and put to death. The one debit in his account is that he exults when he learns that members of the queen's faction have been executed. To that extent, he invites his own downfall. But as a devoted Yorkist, he also shares in the doom of that noble house.

LORD STANLEY, EARL OF DERBY

The stepfather of Richmond moves through a good part of this play cautiously endeavoring to avoid offense to Richard without really committing himself. He offers marked contrast to Hastings, whose sense of well-being he never shares so long as Richard lives. Unlike Dorset and others, he does not cross the seas to join Richmond; he waits to see the ultimate turn of events. Placed in a position where he dares not lead his troops in support of the claimant, he nevertheless survives to witness the fall of Richard II and the crowning of his stepson.

QUEEN ELIZABETH

The wife of Edward IV is from the first a woman who finds no peace. Only briefly does she find a degree of comfort when her dying husband requires members of the quarreling factions to take the vow of amity. But no sooner does she become a widow than her troubles multiply — the news of the executions of her "proud kindred"; the necessity of urging Dorset to flee; the cruel murder of her two young sons. And then there is Queen Margaret to inform her that all this is the working out of divine justice. Aware that the author of her chief woes is Richard III, she still appears to be won over by his facile argument and to agree to the marriage of her daughter to the king. But the subsequent action, wherein it is revealed that the young lady will marry the virtuous Richmond, exonerates her from the charge that she is a "relenting fool, and shallow changing woman."

LADY ANNE

The widow of Edward, Prince of Wales, son of Henry VI, became the wretched wife of Richard of Gloucester. Prior to her appearance in Act I, scene ii, it was from Richard himself that we learned of his villainy. Anne's first function, then, is to provide chapter and verse for Richard's villainy by excoriating him as the heartless murderer of her husband and her father. Yet she is rather easily swayed by Richard's blandishments and agrees to marry him. In a sense, she willfully embraces evil when she accepts Richard as her husband — the man she had just denounced as a "foul devil," "a dreadful minister of Hell." It is not Queen Margaret who is called upon to bring down curses on Anne's head; she does so for herself. And each curse is realized: she does not find rest as Richard's wife; she does not survive long as Richard's queen. Thus, in a way, she expiates her own initial sin.

THE DUCHESS OF YORK

The mother of Edward IV, Clarence, and Richard invites nothing but the deepest sympathy in this play. She has survived the violent deaths of her husband and of her son Clarence; she has seen another son, King Edward IV, languish and die, leaving his realm split with dissension. But the greatest cross she bears is the knowledge that she is the mother of the monstrous Richard: "He is my son — yea, and therein my shame —." Yet when mother and son first exchange words, she cannot deny him the blessing he hypocritically asks for. There is supreme irony and pathos in her words:

> God bless thee, and put meekness in thy mind,
> Love, charity, obedience, and true duty.   (II.ii.107-08)

Nor is this blessing to lead one to assume that the duchess becomes one who is deceived by the arch-villain. It is a heartfelt plea to God that Richard may reform. Old in years and sorrow, she can find sympathy even for that terrifying figure, Queen Margaret, doom of the house of York.

REVIEW QUESTIONS

1. What characteristics peculiar to the Machiavellian villain-hero are revealed in Gloucester's first soliloquy, Act I, scene i?

2. Richard is early referred to as a "hedgehog" and later repeatedly as the "boar." What is the significance of this appellation?

3. In the introduction, reference is made to Senecan elements in this play. What is one example each as regards (a) style, (b) character, (c) theme, (d) tragic elements?

4. In what way are the two wooing scenes (I.ii and IV.iv) similar to each other? How do they differ?

5. What dramatic purpose is served by such minor characters as the three London citizens and the scrivener?

6. Keeping in mind the major theme of this play, how can you account for the fact that the villain-hero flourishes for such a relatively long time?

7. Why is Queen Margaret's appearance in this play unexpected? How do you account for it?

8. What is the first indication that Richard's fortunes, which have been in the ascendant, have reached a turning point? What do you consider to be the climax of the play?

9. George Bernard Shaw insisted that Richard was a splendid comedian. What can be said in support or in refutation of this opinion?

10. According to a long-lived theory, tragedy evokes the tragic emotions of pity as well as fear. What scenes are especially notable for arousing our sense of pity?

11. "In Buckingham we have an admirable foil to Richard." How may one defend this statement?

12. What is meant by dramatic irony? Illustrate your definition by three examples from this play, each differing with regard to the person or persons concerned.

13. Especially since this play is based upon chronicle history, considerable knowledge of antecedent action is needed. Shakespeare does not choose to use a prologue to provide such information. Exactly how, and by whom, is it provided?

14. Since the major theme of this play is God's vengeance visited upon those guilty of heinous crimes, how can one explain the deaths of the queen's kinsmen, Hastings, and the little princes?

15. When the Duchess of York and Queen Elizabeth berate King Richard in Act IV, scene iv, he exclaims:

> Let not the Heavens hear these telltale women
> Rail on the Lord's anointed.

Is this another example of Richard's hypocrisy? Or can he properly call himself the Lord's anointed?

16. Both Richard and Richmond use the name St. George as a battle cry. Why is this appropriate in both instances? Why is it nevertheless ironic that Richard should use the name of St. George?

17. What justification does Richmond have for identifying himself as "God's Captain?"

18. Aside from his "timorous dreams" reported by Anne, what evidence do you find that Richard has begun his descent on Fortune's Wheel?

19. Why is it appropriate that Buckingham should not survive to aid Richmond?

20. In what ways do Lord Stanley (Derby) and Lord Hastings provide an interesting contrast?

21. How does Shakespeare succeed in centralizing the conflict in this play and thus achieve a superior chronicle history play which is also a tragedy?

22. Shakespeare develops the major theme of *Richard III* with unstinted use of the supernatural. What are four examples? Which do you find to be most effective?

23. With reference to the proposal of marriage of her daughter, how may the Queen-Mother Elizabeth's apparent changeableness and double-dealing be explained?

24. More than one reference is made to Jane Shote in this play, although she does not make her appearance. Who was she? In absentia, what does she contribute to the action?

25. On his way to his death, Lord Rivers exclaims against Pomfret, calling it a "bloody prison." Is this to be explained only by reference to his own impending fate? Exactly why is Pomfret truly a "bloody prison"?

SELECTED BIBLIOGRAPHY

Allen, J. W. *A History of Political Thought in the Sixteenth Century,* 1928. Basic to the understanding of Tudor political theories which inform Shakespeare's chronicle history plays.

Berman, Ronald. *A Reader's Guide to Shakespeare's Plays,* 1965. "A discoursive bibliography" which properly includes scholarly articles as well as books relating to *Richard III.*

Boyer, C. V. *The Villain as Hero in Elizabethan Tragedy,* 1914. Contains studies of the Machiavellian "lion and the fox" which anticipates later ones; includes a good presentation of possible influences from Seneca.

Campbell, Lily B. *Shakespeare's "Histories": Mirrors of Elizabethan Policy,* 1947. Penetrating analysis of the religious, ethical, and political ideas in *Richard III:* topical meanings of the play.

Clemen, Wolfgang. *The Development of Shakespeare's Imagery,* 1951. Valuable study of the "formal and artificial" manner modified by a firm architecture of style.

Chambers, E. K. *William Shakespeare: A Study of Facts and Problems,* 2 vols., 1930. Indispensable for bibliographical and historical approach to the play.

Cunliffe, John. *The Influence of Seneca on Elizabethan Tragedy,* 1893. First of the notable studies of this subject; a work which has not become dated.

Furness, H. H., Jr. *Richard the Third.* New Variorum edition, 1908. A storehouse of information including textual criticism, varied interpretations of character and action, stage history.

Kendall, Paul M. *Richard the Third,* 1955. Eminently scholarly and read-
able biography of Richard which provides the essential details relating
to this turbulent period in English history.

Lewis, Wyndham. *The Lion and the Fox,* 1927. Analysis of Richard as the
dedicated Machiavellian.

Marriott, J. *English History in Shakespeare,* 1918. One of the basic studies
of this subject so necessary to an understanding of the chronicle history
plays.

Palmer, J. *Political Characters in Shakespeare,* 1954. Stimulating analysis
of Richard as "brave, witty, resourceful, gay, swift, disarmingly candid,
engagingly sly with his enemies."

Reese, M. M. *The Cease of Majesty,* 1961. Useful discussion of the structure and the language of the play, and of the action in which each successive blow of fate is a fulfillment of a curse until the appearance of
the foreordained savior of England.

Spivack, B. *Shakespeare and the Allegory of Evil,* 1958. Detailed examina-
tion of the morality element in *Richard III.*

Tillyard, E. M. W. *Shakespeare's History Plays,* 1944. Finds *Richard III*
to be an undervalued play; defends the credibility of the play in which
is found a great combination of evil, humor, and artistry in crime.

Study Smart with Cliffs StudyWare®

Cliffs StudyWare® is interactive software that helps you make the most of your study time. The programs are easy to use and designed to let you work at your own pace.

TEST PREPARATION GUIDES
—Prepare for major qualifying exams such as the SAT I or ACT.

• Pinpoint strengths and weaknesses through individualized study plan • Learn more through complete answer explanations • Hone your skills with full-length practice tests • Score higher by utilizing proven test-taking strategies
COURSE REVIEWS—Designed for introductory college level courses.

• Supplement class lectures and textbook reading • Review for midterms and finals

Cliffs NOTES INC. **Get the Cliffs Edge!**

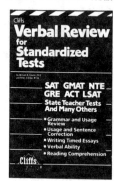

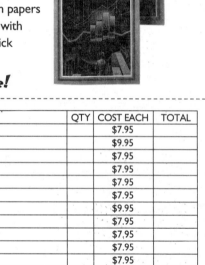

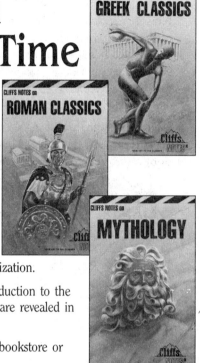